ELEPHANT ON THE HIGH HIMALAYAS

RESURRECTING BHARAT TO FACEOFF CHINA

VETERAN COL RS SIDHU

notionpress.com

INDIA • SINGAPORE • MALAYSIA

Notion Press Media Pvt Ltd

No. 50, Chettiyar Agaram Main Road,
Vanagaram, Chennai, Tamil Nadu – 600 095

First Published by Notion Press 2021
Copyright © Veteran Col RS Sidhu 2021
All Rights Reserved.

ISBN 978-1-63873-657-8

This Book is Dedicated

To my Army coursemates, the Silver Warriors,

And the passionate, young, and vibrant professionals

Who are at the core of the resurgence of Bharat, the new India,

Proud of its past, confident of its future, and willing to stand up for their beliefs.

But for their encouragement and, should I say, insistence,

This book would not have seen the light of the day.

– Veteran Col RS Sidhu

Contents

AN EPISODE FROM
THE REALM OF CONJECTURE

PART I.   THE CONTEXT

PART II.   THE PRESENT

PART III.   THE FUTURE

PART IV.   APPENDICES & BIBLIOGRAPHY

Genesis

In early May 2020 China launched simultaneous incursions across the Line of Actual Control (LAC) at Galwan river valley, Hot Springs and Pangong Tso in Laddakh, and at Naku La in North Sikkim, leading to a standoff with Bharat, the new India.

The resultant chain of events leading to actions of the principals of the Galwan river valley of mid-May 2020 in the high Himalayas, has overturned more than half a century old accommodative policy of erstwhile India along its northern borders, activating geostrategic forces with still unfolding consequences in global time and space.

In Bharat the media 'Battle for TRP' ratings using the modus operandi of 'Breaking News' and the familiar high decibel 'discourse of the experts' brought the standoff into the homes of the common citizens. Lack of official briefings from the Government of the day generated a feeling of leadership vacuum. This left the common citizen confused and concerned as to the truth of the happenings along the northern borders. Heavy psychological warfare by the mighty and infamous propaganda machinery of China began taking its toll. Vested interest groups brought in differing versions of the ongoing impasse to suit their narrative.

It was under these circumstances that some of the aware citizens entered the field to expose the fault lines in the China supported narrative. Having been an amateur 'China watcher' for almost three decades, it motivated me to enter the fray through social media to alleviate some of the concerns amongst fellow citizens within my social reach.

The basic premise of the social media campaign was to focus on facts, keep it simple and short, avoid information overload, present a daily commentary, and create a new racy narrative rather than reacting to the narrative being put forth by the psychological and information warfare establishment of China. For an individual with no organisational resources at command, it entailed a herculean effort to collect, collate, interpret, and disseminate the information in an easily digestible form. It enabled the readers to sift fact from 'true lies' to a great extent!

This also brought me in touch with a broad cross-section of the passionate, young, and vibrant professionals who are at the core of the resurgence of Bharat, and are proud of its past, confident of its future, and willing to stand up for their beliefs.

The relative success of the initiative brought in heavy pressure from the readers to convert the effort into a book form. My response was "…why not as long as you are willing to join in by voicing your thoughts?"

Preface

The hallmark of a natural born leader is the ability under stress to transcend the barriers of fear and conventional wisdom, alike, in undertaking actions capable of causing geostrategic ripples beyond intended space and time.

The twenty-first century is witnessing a monumental 'clash of civilisations' on the high Himalayas, between Bharat – the new India – and China, representing two of the oldest continuous civilisations the world has known. The outcome of this clash shall not only determine the future of a third civilisation, which is Tibetan, but shall also set the geostrategic discourse for the world at large, truly making it the 'Asian Century'.

Bharat and China are a study in contrast. Bharat is democratic, with a federal governance structure and capitalist economy. China on the other hand is essentially a dictatorship, with a state controlled economy. Bharat is a status quo power, whereas China is expansionist. Bharat believes in resolving disputes through bilateral dialogue, whereas coercive diplomacy is the primary dispute resolution mechanism for China.

However it is the world view held by the two cultures which most clearly defines the difference in approach of the two nations. Bharat looks at the world as an interconnected whole, 'Vasudev Kutumbakam' –(the world is one). China, on the other hand, views itself as the centre of the Universe before whom all other countries must kowtow.

A resurgent Bharat is looked at as a key threat by China to realise its ambition of establishing a new Sino-centric world order. A threat that needs to be nipped in the bud, before it becomes too powerful to counteract.

This book looks at the past to search for the root causes of the ongoing geopolitical happenings, explores the current standoff and advances distinctive options for Bharat. But the most interesting and significant aspect of the book is exploring the geostrategic portends in Asia for the 2020-2025 CE period.

'ELEPHANT ON THE HIGH HIMALAYAS' very cogently captures the essence of this ongoing clash between the two oldest and most populous civilisations on earth, representing over one third of all humanity.

Foreword

I am delighted to write this foreword for this timely work written by Veteran Col RS Sidhu titled '*Elephant on the High Himalayas – Resurrecting Bharat to Faceoff China*'. As China's troops laid seige to vast tracts of land in the western sector of the border with India, it is necessary that we study the challenge carefully and provide policy suggestions to counter. Colonel Sidhu has done that ably.

China's military mobilisation in the western sector of the border with India in early 2020 has shattered the modicum of peace on the borders and has set in a new policy orientation in India. The two militaries are mobilised to the hilt even as eight rounds of local commanders' meetings and foreign ministry-led border mechanism consultative meetings have been conducted. An estimated total of over ten divisions have been reportedly mobilised indicating the severity of the situation on the borders. Both countries' leaders have sent signals of resolve.

Such a state of affairs between the two largest countries in Asia by population, economy, standing armed forces, conventional and nuclear capabilities, technological prowess, strategic depth, and demographic dividend suggest a bleak picture for years to come. It also points to the failure of policies of engagement followed by India with China since independence and suggests the complete overhauling of our policies, priorities and strategies vis-à-vis China.

Despite a series of engagement policies such as diplomatic normalisation in 1976 after the 1962 border clashes, commissioning of over 30 structured dialogue processes at various ministerial levels, two 'informal summit' meetings at Wuhan and Chennai, enhancing trade and investments, people-to-people contacts and others, the military-build-up by China had rudely shaken up India.

That 'business-as-usual' with China is not possible is reflected in a series of measures that India took in the aftermath of the killing of 20 Indian soldiers at Galwan on June 15. These range from the ban of IT apps to curbs on investments from China in the infrastructure projects to full-scale mobilisation of the armed forces to counter 'two-front war' and active participation in the resumed four-nation navies' Malabar exercises.

Across the policy spectrum, India has now various options ranging from controlled engagement in multilateralism to a balance of power approach to status quo or even a containment policy, even as it intends to usher in peace and stability on the borders as it existed before April 2020.

All policy options come at a high price to the nation and hence, as the author takes us through the timely and relevant work, need to be clearly laid out and discussed threadbare. All stakeholders need to ponder over these as the nation comes to the crossroads of its security.

The book then offers the policy makers, decision-makers, armed forces, media and the lay citizen the vital discussions on border security, measures to be undertaken to strengthen defences, understand the real intentions of China and take countermeasures.

Colonel Sidhu has painstakingly gone through China's policies, its intentions and capabilities and provided a set of policy options that need to be carefully examined. This book forms a significant value addition to our understanding of the subject. It has been presented in a lucid and cogent manner and is easily readable. More significantly, it is hoped that through this timely intervention, we formulate effective policies to counter China's machinations.

SrikanthKondapalli, Ph D

Professor in Chinese Studies

Centre for East Asian Studies

Jawaharlal Nehru University, New Delhi

Dr Srikanth Kondapalli, a renowned Sinologist, is the recipient of K Subramanyam award by Manohar Parrikar Institute of Defense Studies and Analysis in 2010, and has authored several books on China

China's Military, the PLA in Transition (1st edition). New Delhi: South Asia Books. ISBN 9788186019184.

China's Naval Power. New Delhi: Institute for Defence Studies and Analyses. ISBN 9788186019375.

China and its Neighbours. New Delhi: Pentagon Press. ISBN 9788182744493.

China's Military and India. New Delhi: Pentagon Press. ISBN 9788182746893.

China and the BRICS Setting Up a Different Kitchen(2017 edition). New Delhi: Pentagon Press. ISBN 9788182749276.

One Belt, One Road: China's Global Outreach. New Delhi: Pentagon Press. ISBN 9789386618030.

An Episode from the Realm of Conjecture

> *Bharat's understanding goes beyond
> the conventional concept of Time,
> To comprehend the Cosmic scale of Time,
> Where Kaal can imply
> both Time and Death.*

Chronicle of Kaalraatri

The Rebirth of an Audacious Bharat

*"It is the **life in my men** and not the number of men in my life which matters!" – Marilyn Monroe*

*"In any battle, the imponderable and critical factor is what is going to happen when commanders are exhausted and under extreme pressure and when their **mens' adrenalin is flowing**."*–in 'Red Armour' by Richard Simpkins

Now what do a renowned military theoretician and a probably even more renowned movie star have in common and what does it have to do, post Galwan, with the Chinese threat of a two-front war against Bharat the new India.

Marilyn Monroe must know what she was saying, having been wooed simultaneously by two of the most powerful men of the most powerful country of the world during her time, and the two quoted are talking of the same thing, 'the life in the men,' the major difference between the armed forces of born again Bharat and China – Pakistan.

The Chinese, or for that matter of fact even their allies the Pakistanis, simply lack the soldiers with 'life in them' in adequate numbers, to take on the 'mad breed of ordinary men' found in abundance in the armed forces of Bharat. Occupying vacant heights with special forces, which both China and Pakistan seem to specialise in – a la Galwan and

Kargil – can no way be equated to capturing them in mortal combat.

Bharat's Mad Breed of Ordinary Men

Numbers have seldom determined the course of military history. In post-independence India the courageous defence of Srinagar in 1948, Battle of Asal Uttar in 1965, Battle of Longewal in 1971, and the Battles of Nathu La and Cho La in 1967 are but a few examples where superior leadership, grit, determination and never – say – die spirit of the Indian armed forces carried the day despite being heavily outnumbered and outgunned.

The 'mad breed of ordinary men' of the armed forces of Bharat have proved it at Qaid-e-Azam Post on the forbidding heights adjoining Siachen Glacier, the majestic and bleak Tiger Hill and Tololing heights in Kargil, and Black Top in Laddakh, to name a few! Be it the icy 'Heights of Madness' as Myra Macdonald, the Reuters correspondent, refers to the war on Siachen Glacier, or Wing Commander Abhinandan Varthaman going beyond orders to shoot down an F-16 in an antiquated MIG-21, or the 'mad breed of ordinary men' who on their own bested the best of China in Galwan river valley in May 2020, it runs in the blood.

You have to be mad to capture an occupied post at an altitude of 21,000 feet, after climbing a 1,500 feet vertical ice wall, in pitch darkness, in sub-zero temperatures!

You have to be mad to chase and shoot down an F-16, in an antiquated MIG-21, in a crazy dogfight!!

You have to be mad to **charge barehanded** into enemy positions at Galwan river valley, against thrice the numbers and take down scores of their soldiers!!!

The midnight madness of Galwan river valley galvanised the corridors of power in New Delhi to proactively respond to the threat of a two-front war being bandied about by China and its junior ally Pakistan.

Detailed deliberations led to the most daring operation ever conceived and launched by South Block, New Delhi.

Operation KAALRAATRI 2020

01 JULY – Ministry of Defence (MoD), South Block, New Delhi issues a short press release announcing the holding of routine exercise with troops with two infantry divisions and two armoured brigades in the general area of Pokhran and Mahajan in Rajasthan from 25 August to 25 September.

04 JULY – Meeting of 12 notables, including three of distinct foreign origin, is held at a secluded airbase somewhere along the eastern coastline of Bharat. The meeting commenced at 2100 hours and lasted till 0200 hours. No records were maintained, and the decisions arrived at were stored in cerebral memory.

08 JULY – Bharat and the US Central Command announce the holding of an **amphibious** exercise from 15 August to 10 September, in the Arabian Sea region off the coast of Gujarat.

10 JULY – The US Pacific Command announces holding of a naval exercise from 20 August to 10 September, off the coast of Vietnam adjoining South China Sea (SCS). Naval ships from the US, Japan, Australia, Bharat, France, Vietnam, Philippines, and the UK shall take part to enhance interoperability.

15 JULY – MoD, South Block, New Delhi issues a short press release announcing holding of a joint Air Force exercise from 25 August to 05 September, in the general region of Maharashtra, Rajasthan, Haryana, Madhya Pradesh, Bihar, West Bengal, and Assam. Air Force of Bharat, US, France, and Israel will participate to enhance interoperability and jointmanship.

03 AUGUST – The Tibetan Government-in-exile, located at Mcleodganj in Himachal Pradesh appeals to the international community to take steps to prevent human rights abuses, cultural genocide, and denial of the right to practise religion in Tibet.

14 AUGUST – The UK, Australia, and France call for an urgent discussion by the United Nations (UN) Security Council to discuss Human Rights abuse by China in Tibet and Xinjiang province. China vetoes the proposed UN Security Council resolution.

15 AUGUST

Near simultaneous air attacks are carried out by unidentified drones on the Srinagar airbase in Jammu &Kashmir (J&K) and the Jaisalmer airbase in Rajasthan. Overall seven service personnel are killed and thirteen injured. Light damage to infrastructure is also reported.

Bharat and the US Naval amphibious task forces assemble at the Arabian Sea for joint drills. An Aircraft Carrier from the Bharat Navy heads its task force.

16 AUGUST – Bharat charges Pakistan based terrorist organisations and Inter Service Intelligence (ISI) agency of Pakistan for masterminding the dastardly attack. It declares its resolve to retaliate at a time and place of its own choosing. Pakistan denies the charge vehemently and responds by raising defence alert all along its eastern borders with Bharat.

20 AUGUST – Naval task forces from the eight participating countries assemble off the coast of Vietnam for a joint exercise.

23 AUGUST – The World Health Organisation (WHO) announces the completion of an inquiry into COVID-19 pandemic. The report indicts senior functionaries of WHO and China for negligence and mishandling, resulting in adversely impacting the international effort to prevent its spread. Worldwide calls are made for sanctions against China for committing crimes against humanity.

25 AUGUST – Six squadrons from participating foreign countries land in military air bases in Maharashtra, Rajasthan, West Bengal, and Assam. No flying zones and flight corridors for civilian flights are announced for the duration of the joint exercise. Pakistan places its Air Force on full alert and activates its air defence network.

26 AUGUST – Ministry of External Affairs (MEA) of Bharat conducts a press brief and alleges that electronic and satellite imagery findings unequivocally point to drone attacks being guided from within Pakistan territory. It asserts territorial sovereignty over Pakistan Occupied Jammu & Kashmir (POJK) and Shaksgam Valley and **pronounces for all foreigners to vacate these areas by 30 August**.

27 AUGUST

An emergency meeting of Pakistan Army Corps Commanders is held at their General Headquarters (GHQ).

Director General (DG), ISI in his briefing lays out his assessment that intelligence reports indicating the imminent launch of punitive air operations by Bharat in Azad Kashmir are just part of their deception cover plan and actual attacks are to be conducted by their navy on military installations at Karachi and Gwadar ports.

During ensuing discussions, the dominant view emerges that major presence of Chinese military assets in Azad Kashmir are a strong deterrent to Bharat launching cross Line of Control (LC) operations in that region. Bharat has earlier employed its Army and then the Air Force for conducting two raids across the LC. Extremely reliable human intelligence inputs indicate that this time around Bharat has planned to launch retaliatory naval operations to achieve surprise.

The presence of a strong naval amphibious task force of Bharat in the vicinity of Makran coast, clinches their decision.

The meeting also discussed the option of going proactive, but the alternative was discarded as being foolhardy, keeping in view the heavy foreign air force presence in the airspace of Bharat, and foreign naval assets engaged in amphibious exercises in the vicinity of Makran coastline.

The meeting was adjourned after taking a decision to deploy suitable naval resources along the Makran coast, and transfer of additional air assets from Punjab to Sindh.

28 AUGUST – Vietnam and Philippines announce the recognition of Taiwan as an independent country. China threatens retaliation.

29 AUGUST – Secret parleys are held in Macau, between a distinguished Chinese identified as 'The Elder', and a 'person of influence' from Russia. Personal promises are made and given. Rumours have surfaced from time to time about the existence of a shadowy group of elderly statesmen in China, exercising behind-the-scene influence over government decisions impacting the long-term core interests of China.

30 AUGUST – International Monetary fund (IMF) announces a review of monetary loans to Pakistan, citing violation of terms of the loan agreement.

31 AUGUST

0400 hours – Vietnam and the Philippines occupy uninhabited islands inside the immediate periphery of the Chinese 'nine-dash line' in the SCS, under the cover screen provided by an US-led international naval armada. China announces heavy retaliation if occupation forces do not withdraw from the occupied territory within 48 hours.

1230 hours – Prime Minister Office (PMO) of Bharat announces address by Prime Minister to the nation at 2030 hours.

1900 hours – Heavy air activity off Karachi harbour and in general area of Jaisalmeris reported by the Pakistan air defence network. Pakistan activates combat air patrols for air defence tasks.

1915 hours – All Pakistan air defence radars in Sindh, Baluchistan and Punjab provinces of Pakistan are rendered ineffective by heavy electronic jamming.

2000 hours

The Prime Minister of Bharat addresses the nation and the international community at large.

He announces ongoing air attacks across the LC as retaliation for Pakistan Government sponsored terrorist attacks on Bharat. He also clarifies that cross LC action will be restricted to the use of air assets and reiterates Bharat's commitment to respect the sanctity of the International Boundary.

He further affirms that the armed forces have been given a free hand to respond with full force if Pakistan violates the International Boundary or employs ground force across LC.

He also goes on to publicly address the government of People's Republic of China, reinforcing Bharat's commitment to maintaining peace and tranquillity across the Line of Actual Control (LAC), while asserting Bharat's sovereignty over POJK and Shaksgam region. He states that any Chinese presence in POJK, military or commercial, violates international norms and is unacceptable.

Pakistan – 31 August 2000 hours to 01 September 0600 hours

The foreign air assets present within Bharat flew combat ready 'training' air patrols throughout the night along the western borders of India in Maharashtra, Gujarat, and Rajasthan, and in the depth of northern borders in West Bengal, and Assam in the north-east. This enabled the Bharat Air Force to concentrate its full might in Punjab and J&K to conduct missions across the LC in POJK.

'Operation *Kaalraatri*' had commenced.

Top-secret airborne electronic warfare assets were used to blind the enemy radars and communication networks across the LC.

Airfield runways were the first to be hit and rendered unfit for flying operations.

Pakistan as well as the Chinese Command Control and Communication infrastructure in POJK was rendered inoperative within the first hour of commencement of air operations. This critically hampered their attempted retaliatory operations.

Enemy radars, air defence assets, airfields, logistics infrastructure, terrorist camps, gun emplacements along the LC, and selective surface communication infrastructure in

POJK depth areas were successively targeted throughout the night, by employing air and ground launched precision guided munitions.

All assets of Pakistan Air Force(PAF) and Peoples Liberation Army Air Force(PLAAF) in POJK were destroyed or damaged beyond repair. No airbase in POJK was spared.

Special combat effort was also applied on specific power and commercial projects being undertaken by Chinese organisations and Pakistan military business ventures within POJK.

It was a night of terror, '***Kaalraatri***,' across the LC.

Within minutes of commencement of '*Kaalraatri*', a special package was hand delivered to Pakistan GHQ by the US Military Attaché. It contained transcripts of relevant excerpts of discussions being held in GHQ secret underground command centre. Even more ominous was an accompanying package prominently marked Israel, containing aerial photographs with crosshairs superimposed over all known and secret locations holding nuclear assets of Pakistan.

Commander of the US Central Command, as well as the US Ambassador to Pakistan followed up with urgent consultations over the phone with the Chief of Army Staff, Pakistan Army advising him not to precipitate matters.

With US naval assets deployed on battle stations to the South, off Makran coast, and coalition aircrafts airborne close to eastern borders, the message to Pakistan was very clear.

China - 31 August 2000 hours to 01 September 0600 hours

The great Chinese 'Cyber Firewall' was breached for duration of 13 minutes. Simultaneously, the electronic signals from 13 satellites of the Chinese BeiDou navigational system were also interrupted for 13 minutes. Curiously this was also the exact duration of the erratic communication problem between Beijing and Peoples Liberation Army Rocket Force (PLARF).

The Moscow – Beijing hotline remained active throughout the night. The Russian 'person of influence' and the distinguished Chinese 'The Elder', participants in the 29 August meeting at Macau, also talked over the phone. The Russian 'person of influence' obliquely touched upon the Chinese difficulties in cyberspace as a 'technical glitch' in his conversation with the Chinese 'Elder'. The tacit implication of this indirect message was readily understood by the Chinese.

An emergency and secret conclave of 'The Elders', the shadowy Chinese oligarchy purported to wield real influence in China, was urgently convened. The obliquely conveyed message from the Russian 'person of influence' was presented to the distinguished gathering. The decision reached upon was unanimous.

Beijing reiterated its commitment to maintain the territorial integrity of China, resist external destabilising influences in the region, and to continue to work towards restoring regional peace and harmony. It further announced its commitment to hold bilateral discussions with respective countries to peacefully resolve maritime disputes in the SCS and mutually abjure use of force for resolving the differences.

The Chinese spokesperson also denounced the use of force by Bharat in J&K region and favoured resolving disputes between the neighbours through dialogue in the spirit of mutual give and take.

The spokesperson studiously denied any deployment of Chinese military forces in POJK.

Bharat 01 September 0900 hours

The Defence Minister of Bharat holds a press conference to announce calling off trans-LC air operations as all its aims had been achieved. However, he also warns that the armed forces of Bharat have been ordered to take resolute action against any retaliatory action by an adversary.

Postscript

The international strategic community closely following the operations were left deeply impressed at the successful execution of the masterly deception plan by Bharat.

They even marvelled at the audacity of Bharat in employing its airpower, numerically inferior to its adversaries, to successfully deliver the *coup de main*.

But they were also perplexed by the emerging indirect evidence alluding to unexplained operational capabilities displayed during the conduct of operations!

What was the equipment employed to disrupt radar and communication electronics over such an extended geographical space? Was it one single unit or employed in multiples? Which country was the owner? It had the potential to herald the next revolution in military affairs.

There were also unsubstantiated reports of unexplained structural damages in POJK that could not be attributed to kinetic energy or explosives. The reports, if true, went beyond any known directed energy weapon technology! Shocked survivors, some with severe internal haemorrhage, when interviewed subsequently, could just recall feeling invisible but strong energetic vibrations in the air followed by omni-directional, low, and deep humming noise. They claimed it was the wrath of God! Bharat scoffed at such reports as a product of delusion induced by acute psychological trauma suffered by the victims.

The technology to listen deep was rumoured to exist. But were the transcripts of conversation handed over to GHQ the outcome of this technology or attributable to plain human intelligence resources?

Rumours of service break down of BeiDou navigational system were strongly denied by China.

What else advanced military technologies did exist but were not yet out in the open?

The political leaders of Bharat boasted of the success of the operations to the benign influence of *Mangal* and *Kaali*, the God of war and Goddess of war and retribution, respectively. The existence or employment of the rumoured top-secret weapons was left unsaid!

During the press conference when an Italian press correspondent persisted with his query about Bharat possessing *Kaali*, a directed energy weapon platform, the Raksha Mantri smilingly responded, "Modern science is only now veering around to the fact of 80% of the matter in the Universe being 'dark matter'. One of the more interesting meeting points of Hindu and Roman theology is on the God of War, where very interestingly, both happen to represent the fourth planet of our Solar system, *Mangal* or Mars. But it is the belief in *Kaali,* the Goddess of dark energy and retribution, unique to our theology that makes the difference!"

PART I

The Context

> The Book had long ordained,
> an Elephant will be the Kaal,
> To purge the Dragon from
> the land of Spiritual Taal.
> The Elephant averse to ascend
> the high Himalayas,
> Is thrust to the forefront, to answer
> the Destiny's call.

Chapter I

The Elephant Remembers

> *"It is the armed might for sure which secures the road to peace, Internal dissensions lead only to the path of inevitable defeat."*

Walk Over on the High Himalayas

It is the mailed fist behind the folded hands which ensures peace essential for successfully engaging in trade and commerce.

The decline of Bharat of yore, the proverbial 'Soneki Chidiya' (Golden Bird), commenced with the decline of its military might compared to its flourishing trade and commerce. Consequently, invaders lured by its fabled wealth and weak defence made inroads and ensconced themselves as the dominating power.

India was the world's largest economy with 32.9% share of the world Gross Domestic Produce (GDP) in the First Century CE, 28.9% in the 11th Century CE, and 24.4% in the 17thCentury CE. In perspective, the share of entire Europe in 17th Century CE was 23.3%. By 1947, India's GDP, as a share of the world GDP had shrunk to a mere 3%. (1).

The waning of India's military might can be attributed to the internecine internal feuds leading to no holds barred fratricidal wars. To save on costs during times of peace, the states began maintaining a small core as a standing army. As and when the requirement arose, the state would expand the armed forces through a system of royal title holders who were required to provide a specified quantum of troops for the conduct of military campaigns.

This created the rise of multiple centres of power, distinct from the ruler. Over a period of time, the primary loyalty of the rank file came to lie with the title holder rather than the ruler. This system worked well only as long the central rule was strong and the going was good. It tended to collapse when the state weakened, or the adversary was seen to winning the battle of the day. These courtiers and their troops tended to just melt away in the face of a determined onslaught.

Even then, India came under foreign rule not because the invaders were stronger than it. The country lost due to its internal bickering. All the invaders from Alexander to Babur, to the British East India Company, came in with a force of mere 20,000 to 50,000 soldiers. It is the armed support to the invaders from within that proved to be India's undoing.

The current predicament being faced by India, on the high Himalayas, can be traced to a lack of strategic culture in our system of governance. This flaw was implanted during the British rule and the system of governance adopted by them.

Direct British rule over India lasted for just under a century, from The Crown taking over India from East India Company in 1858 to the grant of independence in 1947. To safeguard their rule over such a vast region the British had to subjugate its will, which they did by a deliberate policy of denigrating India's culture and system of education.

'The Lays of Ancient Rome' is a collection of Roman ballads penned by Thomas Babington Macaulay in the fourth decade of the 19th century while in India. They formed part of the language curriculum of English public schools for the most part of the 19th and 20th century.

It is an irony indeed, that an excerpt from his Roman ballads "…and how can man die better than facing fearful odds, for the ashes of his fathers and temples of his Gods…" even adorns India's Rezangla War Memorial, near Chushul in Laddakh, dedicated to its martyrs of the 1962 war with China.

Such a man of letters and culture would be well aware of the import of cultural moorings to the spirit of a nation.

It was this same Macaulay who through his infamous 'Macaulay's Minutes' propagated "…a need to produce—by English language higher education—a class of persons, Indian in blood and colour, but English in taste, in opinions, in morals and intellect…"

This was the basis of the English Education Act of 1835, the final blow of the sword that would sever Bharat from its cultural roots for the next two centuries.

To assist in keeping the peasantry suppressed at large, the British established an intermediary neo-feudal class '*The Sahibs*', with colonial titles. It laid the foundation of a subservient India, led by the new '*Sahibs*' and '*Sirs*', beholden to the British Empire for their ill-gotten influence and position in return for keeping the 'Indians' subjugated culturally, morally, and politically.

A new and subservient India was created with the active support of these '*Sahibs*' and '*Sirs*'. The erstwhile Bharat became a distant memory.

How well Macaulay succeeded in his designs can be gauged from the fact that even 70 years post-independence we are still fighting the progenies of these '*Sahibs* and *Sirs*', and the neo converts beholden to their 'eco system', to regain our cultural, moral, and political heritage.

No state can survive on mere benevolence. Shorn of niceties, the coercive power of a state is a must for it to survive and thrive. The British established the military as their external coercive arm to extend their dominion, the police as their internal coercive arm to suppress dissent, and the revenue administration machinery as their internal coercive arm for filling their coffers. Even 70 years post-independence this mindset is still visible in our system of local governance and policing.

The Indian Civil Service (ICS), was created as the trusted steel frame, to safeguard the foundations of the British Empire in India. The wily British kept all geostrategic dealings outside the domain of this ubiquitous steel frame. The geostrategic affairs and the military were directly controlled by London through the Viceroy. Thus, there were two parallel hierarchies, the military and the civil. The latter was bereft of experience in handling strategic affairs.

The political class which came to power in India were equally oblivious about strategic culture as their new found advisors the ICS, now redesignated as Indian Administrative service (IAS). The fear of the unknown, actively fuelled by the bureaucracy, led the new political dispensation to downsize and denigrate the military. The military and the harsh truths of geostrategic realities became taboo. A weakened military was, to them, a controllable military and if that went against the national interests, so be it.

One of the most insidious theories propounded to keep the military undermined within the governance structure of the Republic of India has been to periodically raise the bogey of a military coup. India is a mature democracy. In no other mature democracy do we have the poor spectacle where the integrity and loyalty of its armed forces is called into question, time and again.

Prominent strategic and military analysts within the country have expressed their views from time to time, in well-articulated critiques, about the improbability of a military coup in India or rather of it being a non-issue. These thinkers have based their views upon critical aspects of the most rigorous due diligence process followed for selection of the three service chiefs with inputs from multifarious security and intelligence agencies, armed forces to population ratio, plethora of intelligence and paramilitary forces, broad spectrum of regional representation, size and vastness of territorial spread of the country, strong democratic traditions of the nation, and finally, but not the least, the historical track record of political aloofness of the armed forces. These all combined would preclude any eventuality of a military coup.

However, the bogey of a military coup has been kept alive and continues to raise its ugly head from time to time. There is only one plausible answer and its extremely unflattering to the powers at South Block. It is to **keep the**

political class wary of dealing with the armed forces of their own nation!

'The Bogey of Military Coup in India', by the author, is in Appendix 'A' for further reference.

With the military being kept outside the higher structure of governance, in one stroke, the Republic of India was shorn of expert geostrategic advice. The inexplicably varied Indian response to the Pakistan invasion of J&K in 1947-48 and the Chinese annexation of Tibet in 1950-52, adequately highlights the naiveté of the prevailing Indian strategic culture.

India in 1947 was maintaining, in Tibet, a diplomatic mission at Lhasa, trade agency at Gartok, trade and military posts at Gyantse and Yatung, while exercising control over Tibet's post and telegraph network. It is interesting to note that despite overwhelming evidence of Chinese duplicity in Tibet being provided by India's armed forces in the field and her foreign mission in Tibet, the Indian Government of the day declined repeated requests of the Tibetan Government for diplomatic and military support, abandoning Tibet to the marauding Chinese in 1950-52. (2)

The lame excuse of India not being militarily capable of taking on the Chinese in Tibet is just that – a lame excuse. China, during this time period, was embroiled in a war against the US-led UN forces in the Korean peninsula, had voids in infrastructure to employ its air power in Tibet, lacked surface communication to logistically support the size of force which would be required to take on the force which India could deploy in Tibet, and the local population was highly anti-Chinese. India was part of the UN military force fighting against the Chinese in Korea, albeit with a medical field unit only, and the logistic supplies to the Chinese garrison in Tibet during the initial stages of the Chinese occupation of Tibet were being funnelled through India.(2)

In J&K the victorious Indian armed forces were halted in midstride, by the Government of India, and the issue was placed before the United Nations for adjudication. Whereas India was proactive in placing the J&K issue before the UN Security Council, its stand was obverse on the question of Tibet self-determination issue being discussed at the UN. (2)

It is difficult to argue with the exasperated remark by John Kenneth Galbraith, a former US Ambassador to India that "Indians are the world's safest objects of animosity". More so when we look at the ill-thought out strategic decisions leading to the defeat in the 1962 war with China, and outcomes of the 1965 and 1971 conflicts with Pakistan, wherein the hard fought gains of the Indian armed forces were frittered away during the course of diplomatic resolutions of these conflicts.

It is this void in a strategic culture that resulted in the Elephant giving a walk over to the Dragon in the high Himalayas.

Living in Awe of the Dragon

The Battles of the Mind are more difficult to win and have a longer-lasting impact than the physical war.

Marginalised by the state post-independence, military hierarchy trifled with at-will, ground operations remote-controlled from Delhi, the ill-equipped and numerically inferior Indian Army was out-generalled and out-manoeuvred by the Chinese on the high Himalayas in 1962.

Such was the psychological impact on South Block, that even more than half a century later the 'Henderson Brookes-Bhagat' report on the 1962 debacle has not been made public. The political dispensation in power has changed, the military leaders have changed, but the decision to keep the report under wraps has not changed. Only one common factor remains, the bureaucracy responsible for the defence of the country, as per its own rules of business. They are the same; faceless, unaccountable, devoid of geostrategic nuances, and yet unwilling to learn!

The ground troops who bore the physical brunt of the Chinese onslaught, were swift to recover, as is borne by the events of 1965 against Pakistan and 1967 against China. But the bureaucracy remained in shock and awe of China for well over half a century. Do not rock the Chinese boat, became their mantra for survival. Instructions to the troops on the ground were very clear on this aspect, who found it humiliating at most times when face to face with their opponents.

Till a decade back, a visit to the western and northern borders of India highlighted a very subtle but revealing aspect which to the trained eye discloses the psyche of the decision makers of the nation. All along the western borders there are broad black-topped roads leading to nowhere on the borders, whereas across the border there are mere dirt tracks for the initial 10 to 20 kilometres, but for a few exceptions. On the northern borders the situation is reverse. It is glaring evidence, if one was ever needed, of the mindset of the inhabitants of South Block, where such decisions are made!

China is aware of this aura of overwhelming power which they exercise over the minds of South Block and have felt emboldened by this knowledge to grab strategic space along the undefined borders with India through a carefully crafted policy of systematic deceit. China has been frequently encroaching on India's territory at irregular intervals. When India protested, they would withdraw from some and retain some. This policy of creeping annexation of undemarcated territory with India is the primary reason why China, despite 40 years of ongoing border resolution talks, has consistently refused to exchange maps recording its territorial claims along the disputed borders.

It was somewhere around the turn of the 21st century that the strategic shift started taking shape from India's fixation on Pakistan, to a greater focus on the threat along its northern borders. Nathu La in 1967, Sumdorong Chu in 1987, and even reactivation of Daulat Beg Oldie (DBO) airfield in 2008, were mere milestones, where China was successfully checkmated more because of the military leaders who influenced the events through sheer force of their personalities, than a programmed shift in India's stance.

It was only during the standoff at Doklam, Bhutan in 2017 when China for the first time came face to face with the new India that is Bharat. The Chinese were proactively checkmated there. Galwan valley and Chushul in Laddakh in mid-2020 is the confirmatory stamp on the return of the Elephant at the gates of Tibet. The initial steps were diffident but the gallant actions of the military, vociferously backed by the new Bharat, enforced a change in the old narrative being imposed by South Block.

Here, it would be relevant to study two seemingly unconnected developments in 2019, which together highlight the **paradigm shift in Bharat's declared geostrategic intent**.

The first is the incorporation of a vision statement in the Budget 2019-20, presented on 05 July 2019, to **make Bharat a US Dollar 5 trillion economy by 2024-25**. This push in the economy will necessitate greater reach into the markets of volatile regions of East Asia, West Asia, Central Asia, Africa, and the established markets of Europe and the Americas. This will involve securing its market access as well as ensuring the safety of its trade and commerce over extended maritime trade routes. Bharat currently lacks the economic muscle to develop strategic reach to safeguard its economic interests beyond the immediate neighbourhood.

The second development is the **creation of the post of CDS and Department of Military Affairs** (DMA) under the MoD effective from 01 January 2020. Together the two developments **signal the political resolve** of the establishment to distance itself from the hitherto fore reactive policy of a status quo power, attain super-power status in its economy, and simultaneously **upgrade its combat power to proactively deter potential adversaries** from direct interference in its economic endeavours and territorial integrity.

Bharat also has an 'unfinished business of Partition' with Pakistan, inherent in the 22 February 1994 resolution of the Parliament, unequivocally stating the entire state of J&K as an integral part of Bharat and calling upon Pakistan to vacate its illegal occupation of POJK. Chinese occupation of Aksai Chin in the 1950s and illegal ceding of Shaksgam Valley by Pakistan to China in 1963, both territories being part of the undivided J&K, inter alia interject China alongside Pakistan into potential conflict with Bharat. This implies a two-front war threat and could theoretically provoke a proactive strike from the adversaries.

It is surprising, therefore, that financial allocations by the Government to equip its armed forces to meet this enhanced threat have been inadequately planned. This exposes a critical gap between political intent and executive action and puts a question mark on the efficacy of Bharat's geostrategic superstructure. Failure to correctly anticipate Chinese intentions in northern Laddakh in 2020, despite the hindsight of Chinese actions at Doklam in 2017, too is worrisome. It's a weakness that needs to be addressed urgently by Bharat's new strategic custodians.

China is a practitioner of coercive diplomacy and can be dealt with successfully only from a position of strength. It is also a leading practitioner of asymmetric warfare. **Hence, Bharat's geopolitical interface with China needs to cater for a conflict escalation matrix in the spectrums of new-age-technology, cyberspace, space, maritime, insurgency, and conventional spheres.**

Clearly, the current security superstructure has not been able to change with the times and needs a major overhaul.

It has taken us 70 plus years to bring back the military into our higher structure of governance, with the setting up of the DMA under the MoD in January 2020. The results are already there to see. Bharat held onto the gains achieved in Laddakh during the mid-2020 standoff with China, as it was the military which was leading the talks.

There is now no going back for the Elephant, as it would be tantamount to political *hara-kiri*. The stage is set for the real battle of supremacy between the Elephant and the Dragon and the geostrategic discourse between the two shall determine the course of events for decades to come in Asia and beyond.

Chapter II

The Nature of the Dragon

It is natural for a dragon to breathe fire,
As it is for a snake to be venomous.

Geographical Vulnerabilities
of China

China's Neighbourhood

China is bordered to its south by the South East Asian countries of **Vietnam** and **Laos** followed by **Myanmar**.

To its south-west, China is bordered by **Bharat, Bhutan, Nepal, POJK** and **Afghanistan** across the Himalayas and the Tibetan plateau.

To its west lie the Central Asian countries of **Tajikistan, Kazakhstan,** and **Kirgizstan**.

Mongolia and **Russia** border China on the north with **North Korea** bordering it to the north-east.

China's more than 14500 kilometres long coastline on the east and south-east overlooks the Yellow Sea, East China Sea and SCS, the Philippines, Vietnam, Brunei, and Malaysia.

The Buffer Regions of China

There are thick tropical forests on its south-east.

Very high mountains of the Tibetan plateau and Xinjiang dominate its south-west and west boundaries.

Cold desert and arid grasslands of Inner Mongolia and Manchuria are located on its northern boundaries.

The northern, western and south-western border regions of China are arid, having less than 40 centimetres of annual precipitation. The forbidding landscape, very harsh climate and limited rainfall makes these regions inhospitable for human habitation and agriculture.

The border regions provide an effective natural barrier or buffer for land access to the mainland of China.

Vast seas to its east provide the easiest access to the mainland China.

The Core of China

Encompassed by the formidable physical barriers of its frontier regions lies the mainland of China. It comprises of fertile river plains and lowlands in its east and south-central regions and has good precipitation.

The core of China is well served by two great rivers, the **Yellow River** in the north, and the **Yangtze** River to the south. These rivers originate from the Tibetan plateau.

The drainage-basins of these two rivers, though forming just 22% of its landmass, are home to 60% population of China.

Pearl River, the second largest river of China, also originates in the Tibetan Plateau.

Key Geographical Factors

The Tibetan Plateau is the source of three of the largest rivers of China, the **Yellow River** to the north, **Yangtze** River in the centre, and **Pearl River** to the south. Rivers

Indus, **Sutlej**, and **Brahmaputra**, three of the largest rivers of Bharat, too originate from the Tibetan Plateau. Indus river is also the major source of water for Pakistan. Three of the largest rivers of Myanmar and South-East Asia, the **Irrawaddy**, **Salween**, and **Mekong**, also have their origins in Tibetan Plateau. **Tibetan plateau is, thus, critical to the water security of China, Bharat, Pakistan, and South-East Asia.**

Sedimentary deposits in the riverbeds of its major rivers result in repetitive floods, cause for major loss of lives and economic resources.

Tibetan mountain ranges of Great Himalayas, Karakoram, Kunlun, and Tien Shan restrict Chinese land access to the Indian Ocean, making land trade economically prohibitive.

High elevations, sharp slopes, extremely cold climate, low precipitation, distance from the coast all combine to make the western regions relatively unviable for agrarian and industrial commerce. Despite its vast geographical stretch, only 15% of China's land surface is suitable for cultivation. This poses challenges for self-sufficiency in food grains.

Despite an extended coastline, China's access to the open seas is restricted. South Korea and Japan lying across the Yellow Sea dominate Chinese access to the open seas from the north-east. Japan and Taiwan dominate its access to open seas across the East China Sea.

China's access to open seas across the SCS is dominated by Taiwan, Philippines, and other South East Asian countries.

SCS is spread over three and a half lakh square kilometres with an average depth of less than 4000 feet. The SCS contains over 250 small islands, atolls, shoals, reefs, and sandbars, many of which are partially or permanently submerged. This maritime region is rich in natural energy resources and is assessed to have 11 billion barrels of oil and 190 trillion cubic feet of natural gas. It is also the maritime trade lifeline of China. An overall 3.37 trillion US Dollar worth of world maritime trade is transiting through it, including 30% of world maritime oil trade, as per US Energy Information Administration report dated 7 February 2013. Passage of enormous volumes of maritime shipping through its restricted maritime channels, that are safe for large ships, poses difficulties.

The main maritime passage between China-SCS and the Indian Ocean passes through the Strait of Malacca. It is 800 kilometres long and a mere 2.5 kilometres at its narrowest point, requiring 20 hours of transit time. It also has extensive swathes of shallow seas and sub-surface atolls. About **60 percent of China's maritime trade transits through the strategic choke point of the Strait of Malacca,** making it extremely vulnerable to interdiction.

Demographic Vulnerabilities of China

China is actually a relatively narrow country, with an extremely dense population.

The overall population of China is 1.4 billion, but with a highly uneven geographical spread. 60% of its population is concentrated in just 22% of its land mass.

Disparate Demographic Concentrations

Its eastern and south-central regions, forming the core, have an approximate population of 770 million with an average population density of approximately 430 per square kilometre.

South-western region, comprising Tibet has an approximate population of 190 million with an average population density of 80 per square kilometre.

North-western region, comprising Xinjiang, has an approximate population of 100 million with an average population density of 30 per square kilometre.

Northern region, comprising Inner Mongolia, has an approximate population of 160 million with an average population density of 105 per square kilometre.

North-eastern region, comprising Manchuria, has an approximate population of 110 million with an average population density of 140 per square kilometre.

Population is most sparse in the mountainous, desert, and grassland regions of the north-west and south-west. In Inner Mongolia Autonomous Region, portions are completely uninhabited.

Core of China

60% of China's population concentrated in a roughly 1000 kilometres wide arc along the seacoast represents the idea that is China and is overwhelmingly of Han ethnic origin. This arc, containing almost a billion people, is one of the most densely populated regions of the world.

Social Divides

There are pronounced divides within the Han Chinese:-

Urban – rural

Rich – poor

Northern plains – Southern plains

The diversity of these group interests within Han China has frequently led to fragmentation and civil war.

Ethnic Divide

91% of China's population is of Han ethnic origin. The remainder 9% are ethnic minorities.

The next largest ethnic groups in terms of population include the Zhuang – 17 million, Manchu – 10 million,

Hui – 10 million, Miao – 9 million, Uighur – 9 million, Yi – 9 million, Tujia – 8 million, Mongols – 6 million, Tibetans – 6 million, Buyei – 3 million, Yao – 3 million, and Koreans – 3 million.

The strength of ethnic minorities is nearly 100 million, sizable numbers to have, with questionable affinity to the central government.

The Dilemma of Managing Buffer Zones

Geographically a major part of what we think of as China is not ethnically Chinese. Interestingly, whereas the core of China is overwhelmingly Han, the buffer regions are predominantly of diverse ethnicity, with major security connotations.

The thinly populated buffer regions of Tibet, Xinjiang, Inner Mongolia, Qinghai, and Gansu comprise 55% of the country's landmass but contain only 7% of its population. Many of these minorities have doubtful loyalty to China, strained relations with the central government, and active cross-border ties with neighbouring countries.

There also exists a religious divide between the core of China and its buffer regions. The Tibetans are Buddhists, and the Uighurs in Xingjian follow the Muslim faith. Roughly 60% Han population officially are atheists, while the balance believes in various forms of folk religion.

To overcome its perceived security concerns the Chinese Government is implementing a policy of altering the long-term demographic pattern of the outlying regions through the coercive settlement of Han Chinese. The

Han Chinese being relocated in this inhospitable terrain is unhappy and there is a high rate of withdrawal amongst them. This is further alienating the people of its border regions.

Though the Tibet region is now dominated by Han Chinese, it is potentially unstable and is vulnerable to outside influences. Similarly, the Xinjiang region is also now dominated by Han Chinese, whereas the ethnic population of Xinjiang was predominantly Muslim, with a significant ongoing insurgency. Mongolia and Manchuria regions are stable, and of all the four buffers, Manchuria is the most integrated with the Chinese core.

Prominent Demographic Challenges

Due to geographical limitations of inhospitable terrains and climate, the western regions of China have always been at a severe economic disadvantage vi-a-vis the eastern regions. The shift from the traditional agrarian economy to an industrial economy has further sharpened the economic and social divides within China. The demands of an exceptionally high industrial economic growth have fuelled new population concentrations in coastal metropolises on the one hand and increased income disparity between the rich and poor on the other.

The income disparity between the rich and poor in metropolises is increasing and causing social unrest and is one of the most dangerous fault lines within China. The income disparities between eastern and western regions, and the urban and rural areas within them, is causing infrastructure imbalance and adversely impacting the quality of life of the inhabitants.

A major resource allocation dilemma is being posed by the ageing population profile. Population migration in pursuit of economic opportunities is leading the younger age demographic population from the hinterland to the eastern coastal regions. This has created disparate ageing profile in the interiors and the coastal regions. The resource rich coastal states have a comparatively younger age demographic, whereas the states lying in the resource poor hinterland are saddled with a higher age demographic. Allocation of resources for social safety infrastructure for the ageing population is therefore a major concern and a friction point between the states and the centre.

Economic Vulnerabilities of China

The past two decades have witnessed a very high growth rate of the Chinese economy bringing fundamental structural changes. Manufacturing industry concentrations have become the leading growth engine of the new Chinese economy. This has given rise to highly dense population centres along the coastal region, with floating population, creating a new demographic challenge for the central authorities.

Geographical and logistical constraints make manufacturing activity in the hinterland uncompetitive in international trade. The demands of competitive industrial output and international trade have forced China to locate its most vital assets in its exposed maritime underbelly of the coastal regions, making it extremely vulnerable to external threat. China has sought to respond to this dilemma by creating a unilateral maritime buffer zone on the seas along its coastline, bringing a paradigm shift in China's geostrategic challenge of managing its external security.

But this aggressiveness is by itself the major cause of its geostrategic entanglement driving it into conflict with major powers and strong regional markets, as also rising opposition to its Belt and Roads Initiative (BRI), the projected engine of its future economic growth.

Maritime trade and commerce are now critical to China's survival as an economic superpower, making the economy increasingly vulnerable to external influences and resources. The rising economy has also created an acute dependency on foreign resources, especially energy.

China's huge budgetary deficit, state government indebtedness to the public sector, current account deficit, and increasing social security burden on account of an ageing population, is creating rising pressures on its economy making it increasingly vulnerable to external influences. The first impacts will be visible on its BRI projects, the vehicle for its global ambitions.

But the parameter which has the potential to rise to be the biggest fault line within the Chinese economy is Xi Jinping's consolidation of hold over the Chinese Communist Party (CCP) and tightening its grip, under his unchallenged leadership, over the various organs of the state. Ensuring continued domestic grip of the CCP over the country, has led Xi Jinping to tighten controls over the economy. His policy of incentivising the State-owned enterprises, akin to public sector units of Bharat, at the expense of private sector and imposing greater party control over the latter has brought him into conflict with the private sector which already has a major 60% share in China's economy. (3) Equally important from the perspective of the CCP is that the private sector employs 80% of China's workforce. Previous attempts to downsize the private sector started inducing an economic downturn forcing policy backtracks. The CCP is acutely sensitive to any weakening of the economy owing to its impact in raising domestic discontent against the party. It can ignore the large new middle class only at its own peril. On the other hand, rising private sector role in the economy has all the ingredients to create a powerful entrepreneurial lobby that may grow beyond control of the Party. (4)

Xi Jinping's rise to unchallenged authority is founded on his pursuing the path of leading China to global dominance, for which economic supremacy is imperative. He is already facing opposition from rival ideologues on the indefinite extension of his national leadership role from earlier term-based leadership, and of pushing China to challenge the powerful Western bloc prematurely, which may jeopardise the formers' global vision. The inability to rein in the private sector may aggravate internal dissensions to the supremacy of Xi Jinping. The ongoing Chinese Government crackdown against prominent private sector leaders is an indicator of this internal struggle within the CCP (5) and is bound to have a profound impact on the economic performance of China.

Strategic Vulnerabilities of China

China today is one of the major global powers in terms of geopolitical influence. Certainly, in its near vicinity, it strides like a colossus, or, so it seems to the untrained eye. Looked at critically, deep geographical, demographic, economic, and strategic fault lines exist in China.

It lacks 'reckonable' allies, as North Korea and Pakistan do not meet the criteria of being 'reckonable'.

Countries inimical to its desired global image block its maritime aspirations – formidable combine of countries such as USA, Japan, and Bharat by virtue of their geographical locations/maritime power. China's blue water navy despite being the largest navy, in terms of the number of ships, is yet inadequate for the security of its sea lines of communication (SLOC) beyond SCS.

China's maritime dilemma is evidenced by it being forced to undertake US Dollar 800 billion gambles in BRI. China's BRI and ongoing actions in SCS should be seen not as its strength but as its acceptance of its maritime vulnerability. The much vaunted 'String of Pearls' strategy provides it with maritime bases for just peacetime security. Its efficacy to withstand the rigours of active operations, to say the least, is doubtful.

The ongoing debilitating trade war with the US is severely straining its economy.

However, the above also undeniably verifies China's push for a China-centric world, the basic thrust of its deep-rooted national aspiration for centuries.

Maritime Factor

Geography has gifted to China its biggest geostrategic dilemmas, a classic case of being hemmed in 'Between the Devil and the Deep Sea'.

The massive geographical barriers to its North-South-West provide China strategic buffer from external threat. But they also make land trade prohibitively uneconomical and vulnerable as it passes through regions that are politically unstable and volatile.

On other hand, the 14,500 kilometres long coastline provides it access to open seas, critical for China to survive as a major economic and geostrategic powerhouse. But its main SLOC to the Indian Ocean region passes through strategic choke points making it vulnerable to maritime threat. Its major rival, the US, is the pre-eminent maritime power dominating China's maritime trade routes in the Pacific and Indian Oceans.

As the seas to the east provide the easiest access to the mainland of China, it is engaged in creating a maritime buffer zone along the seas by constructing artificial islands on the submerged reefs and atolls and fortifying them. This has brought it into conflict with its seven maritime neighbours and their ally the US.

SCS, in particular, has provided China with answers to two of its critical vulnerabilities, while being its biggest security paradox. Developing and fortifying artificial islands in the SCS has at one stroke enabled it to secure critical energy resources, extend its maritime claim line and Exclusive Economic Zone (EEZ), and create an extended maritime buffer zone.

While this action has enabled China to deter any threat to its economic and political core from the east, it has brought it into conflict with almost all its maritime neighbours, thereby opening the doors to US interference and providing cause for Bharat and Japan to realign them alongside the US to thwart Chinese bellicosity.

The ongoing sapping trade war between China and the US and the maritime standoff between the two in SCS has the potential of blowing into a military confrontation. In such an eventuality, win or lose, Chinese maritime trade will be the first casualty. This by itself is likely to lead to internal instability and give rise to fissiparous forces against central rule. (6)

Chinese propensity to use force or threat to use force has created an antagonistic relationship with two other major Asian powers, Bharat, and Japan. With an aim to secure its northern and south-western flanks, China has propped up North Korea and Pakistan as nuclear armed states with a view to neutralising Japan and Bharat, respectively. It also gives it leverage against the US by diverting the latter's energy and attention towards nuclear proliferation.

This strategy is now unravelling. The Chinese threat has forced Japan to shed its 70 years old policy of pacifism and commence rearmament. In Bharat, a right-wing nationalist party government has hardened its stand against Chinese threats and shifted focus to its northern borders against China, with strategic support from USA. An informal alliance between the US, Bharat, and Japan has the probability to mature into the worst nightmare for China.

BRI and String of Pearls Strategy

China is attempting to overcome this dilemma by exercising two options. The first is to open economic corridors or land trade routes to energy producing regions in West Asia and Central Asia, the BRI. The second is to establish a permanent naval presence along its SLOC, the 'String of Pearls' strategy. The strategies are inherently flawed and should be seen as a measure of China's acceptance of its maritime vulnerability.

The China Pakistan Economic Corridor (CPEC) across Tibet Plateau to Gwadar port on Makran coastline is vital to Chinese interests as an alternative access to the Indian Ocean maritime trade routes. The CPEC passes through the disputed POJK region and the insurgency prone Sindh and Baluchistan provinces of Pakistan. CPEC is within easy strategic reach of India, hence, prone to interdiction in times of hostilities. Similar is the case with the China Myanmar Economic Corridor (CMEC).

The economic corridor to Central Asian and West Asian regions shall pass through the volatile Xinjiang province and the highly volatile Central Asian republics. With a strong US presence in West Asia, it will again be vulnerable to interdiction during hostilities.

The current projected cost of these enterprises is estimated at US Dollar 800 billion and given the survivability, it reflects a measure of desperation for China to come out of its geostrategic dilemma.

The 'String of Pearls' is equally unviable as its efficacy to withstand an openly hostile environment is questionable as China does not have the maritime resources to control the SLOC passing through the Pacific Ocean and the Indian Ocean bottlenecks dominated by Japan, Bharat, and the US. (7)

Orientation of Chinese Armed Forces

The Chinese armed forces are the biggest bulwark against any internal threat to CCP rule, as also the biggest threat to their continuity in power. Hence supreme control over the Chinese armed forces lies with the CCP. This supremacy is ensured through political interface at all levels down to the unit. The command supremacy lies with the political commissars. Curbing initiative is therefore a political imperative. Hence, conformist attitude and political indoctrination in the army hierarchy get priority over professionalism. (8)

The primary responsibility of the armed forces is therefore to safeguard the political hierarchy from its own people. Safeguarding the borders from external threat is secondary. This inhibits the Chinese armed forces from developing their full combat potential against external adversaries. Joint warfare command and control structures, vital for the success of overseas military operations, are inadequately organised owing to the above reasons.

Chinese military is primarily a conscript based force with a minimum of four years of compulsory military service. It lacks combat experience and technological expertise at the grassroots level, and is, therefore, unable to exploit the full potential of modern weapons and technology under battle conditions. (9)

Being sole earning members of the family, the majority of soldiers are reluctant to undertake physical risks. (8) The above factors impact the combat efficiency of its armed forces and their effectiveness beyond the immediate vicinity of its borders are uncertain.

'Understanding China', by the author, is in Appendix 'C' for further reference.

Chapter III

Vision of the Dragon

The Chinese World Vision

The fine line separating an audacious vision from dreams is the intensity of plans and tenacity in pursuit!

The Collective Psyche of China

China has a legacy of almost two thousand years old tradition to view itself as the centre of the Universe. For centuries, China has regarded herself as the Central Flowery Kingdom, the only 'Civilisation' on Earth, and its ruler as T'ien-Tzu, the Son of Heaven. All the Chinese leaders from Sun Yat-Sen, Chiang Kai-Shek, Mao Tse-Dong, Deng Xiaoping, down to present day Xi Jinping share this unshaken belief in the greatness of China and have continuously pursued a compulsive urge to reassert China's imperial grandeur.

In fact, it was Sun Yat-Sen, rather than the communists as popularly believed, who first advocated that China assume a greater responsibility towards the world by articulating "...... we must aid the weaker and smaller peoples and oppose the Greater Powers of the World... Then we will be truly governing the state and pacifying the world".

The Chinese continue to view their country as the fulcrum around which geopolitics must revolve. A strong and confident China must hold sway over all the regions ever part of China or under Chinese suzerainty at any point of history. It is this historic urge, embedded deep into the collective Chinese psyche, which to a great extent explains their inability to peacefully adjust in the established international geostrategic arena.

Fusion of Traditional and Communist Ideology

The occupation of China in quick succession, first by Western powers and then by Japan, at the turn of the 20th century, set off deep national frustration at the inadequacy of the traditional Confucian ideology and socio-political system to cope with the powerful challenge from the West.

Democracy was perfunctorily tried but failed as it could not fit into the traditional Chinese framework.

The Chinese search for a new ideology then turned to Communism. It had many important elements of the traditional Chinese socio-political order. A centralised regime armed with a conformist ideology and a universal vision also carried with it the promise of restoring China its traditional universal role.

Adoption of Communism for Advancing China's National Aims

The communist movement grew under the shadow of growing resentment against the Western powers and Japan and led to an outgrowth of nationalist spirit amongst the Chinese people.

The communist success against the Guomindang government was in no small measure due to their skilful propaganda denigrating the Nationalist Party as a stooge of imperialism. The Chinese Communists thus largely conceived their struggle in nationalist terms aimed at China's regeneration.

Infact, Mao's ascendancy in the Communist movement represented the triumph of the nationalist aspect of communism and the subsequent break by Communist China from the Russian led Communist International movement, further emphasises it.

Today there is seamless fusion between communism and nationalism within China. The concomitant one-party rule ensures ideological continuity and unhindered long-term planning to attain their geostrategic aim of a China centric world order.

'Thrust & Logic of Chinese Foreign Policy', by the author, is in Appendix 'B' for further reference.

Rise of Modern China

It was in 1949 that CCP, led by Mao Zedong, came into power in China after defeating the Chiang Kai Shek led Guomindang Government. By 1950 China, with material support from USSR, had already thrown its weight behind North Korea against the US-led UN coalition forces. The Chinese forces were able to fight the US-led UN coalition forces to a standstill.

It has taken China seven decades to arrive on the world stage as a challenger to the dominant superpower, the US. This rise of China has broadly followed four stages.

Strategic Consolidation

During the first stage, the Chinese leadership focused itself on strategic consolidation. This phase extended over two and a half decades, upto the mid-seventies.

During this period, the CCP led by Mao Zedong consolidated its hold over all organs of the State. Any dissidence to the ruling elite within the CCP was also ruthlessly exterminated. Even while the CCP focused on political consolidation it did not lose sight of its ultimate goal of establishing a China-centric world order.

In 1953 China launched its first five year plan to rebuild its civil war-ravaged economy, with technical support from USSR. Its relative success emboldened Chinese leadership to aim at enhancing its agricultural produce and industrial production to world levels. The plan, launched in 1958 and termed the 'Great Leap Forward', ended in failure and had to be given up after it led to the death of 30 million of its citizens due to famine.

On a parallel track, in pursuit of its single-minded goal of world domination, China instituted a nuclear weapons program in 1955, with initial technical assistance from USSR. However, after the withdrawal of USSR technical assistance in 1959, the nuclear program with designation 'Project 596', was developed indigenously and fructified by 1964 with the detonation of its first nuclear weapon device at Lake Lop Nor nuclear weapon testing site in Xingjian province.

1963 was also the time when Zhou Enlai, the then Chinese Premier first mooted the 'Four Modernisations' plan to modernise the agriculture, industry, defence, and science & technology sectors of the economy with a view to bringing China onto the world stage. But its implementation got side-tracked owing to ensuing internal upheavals.

By this time, the Chinese leadership was disillusioned at having to be a junior partner to the Soviet Communist Party, and with the receding of the geostrategic threat from the US, decided to chart their own nationalist course. The ensuing breakup with USSR led to the withdrawal of technical support by the latter in modernising Chinese industrialisation. This brought an end to the first Chinese attempt to modernise itself to world standards.

Mao Zedong then launched the 'Great Cultural Revolution', to consolidate the hold of the CCP on all organs of the State as also to curb dissidence to his leadership. The period from mid-sixties to mid-seventies was lost to the resultant large-scale purges in Government and its armed forces, as also forced shift of population to agricultural and industrial collectives. A great 'Bamboo Curtain' was dropped to seclude domestic China from external influence and protect its nascent industry from foreign competition.

The most interesting facet is that the internal focus did not deter China from employing coercive force to assert her dominance in the geostrategic neighbourhood during this period.

Tibet was annexed forcefully in 1950.

Employed the PLA in support of North Korea and fought the US-led UN coalition forces to a standstill in Korea in 1951-53.

Launched a border war against India in 1962.

Conducted punitive border action against India at Nathu La in 1967.

Fought with USSR armed forces over Ussuri River Island in 1968.

Supported North Vietnam with armed forces volunteers and logistics in its guerrilla war with the US in the sixties and early seventies.

Forcibly occupied island territory of Vietnam in Paracel Islands, South China Sea in 1974.

Conducted punitive border action against Vietnam in 1979.

The Chinese also showed their geostrategic pragmatism by joining the UN in 1971 and carrying out rapprochement with the US in 1972, while still engaged in an indirect guerrilla conflict against the latter in Vietnam.

Capacity Development through Four Modernisations

The demise of Mao Zedong in 1977 and the emergence of Deng Xiaoping as the leader of CCP in 1978 also signalled the commencement of the second stage of the process to make China a world power. The CCP had by now consolidated its grip over the Chinese state and it felt confident to carry out internal and economic market reforms to initiate capacity development.

Under the guidance of Deng Xiaoping, the Third Plenum of the Eleventh Central Committee held in

December 1978 adopted the Four Modernizations plan, formally marking the beginning of these reforms. The fields of Agriculture, Industry, Defence, and Science & Technology were to be the focus of the Four Modernisations. The basic premise of the Four Modernisations was to develop the capacity to match the Western powers in economic strength and technological advancement to make China a great power.

This was coupled with the gradual and controlled opening of the economy to foreign trade and investment, permitting limited private ownership of the business to its citizens, creation of Special Economic Zones along coastal areas, and approaching multilateral funding and development agencies for funds and technology. By 2005, the private sector had grown to account for 70% of China's GDP, 400 of the Fortune 500 companies had set up operations in China by 2006, and its GDP as a share of world GDP percentage rose from 1.8% in 1980 to 3.97% by 2005.

The setting up of Special Economic Zones along the coastline resulted in the coming up of manufacturing and trade hubs. This increased the strategic importance of the SCS maritime region. China, with a continued eye on its world vision, focused its expansionist policies in the SCS by forcible occupation of island territory in Spratley Islands, from Vietnam in 1988, and occupation of Mischief Reef, from the Philippines in 1995.

Jiang Zemin, who succeeded Deng Xiaoping in 1993, continued with the policy focus laid by the latter.

Regional Pre-Eminence

China entered the third stage of its quest for global dominance with the ascendancy of Hu Jintao in 2003, as a successor to Jiang Zemin. China now focused on developing industries associated with modern technologies and was instrumental in crafting the policy to establish large Chinese corporations with full state support to compete against foreign MNCs.

By 2010 China's GDP had grown to US Dollar six trillion making it the second largest economy after the US. More interestingly its share of the world GDP had risen to 12.5%, it had accumulated a trade surplus of US Dollars 184 billion and was poised to be the largest producer of manufactured goods in the world. (10)

In the geostrategic field China started increasing its dominance by force over the SCS maritime region. The groundwork was laid for the development of a powerful ocean going navy commensurate with its global trade interest. China began to deploy its ships for anti-piracy operations in the Gulf of Aden and established a military base in Djibouti to expand China's influence in Africa and maintain security of its SLOC in the Indian Ocean region.

World Domination

The transfer of leadership to Xi Jinping in 2013, coincided with China emerging as a dominant economic powerhouse with modern armed forces. Under Xi Jinping, China has launched a challenge to the US dominance in both geostrategic and economic spheres, to enter the fourth stage of its aim to be the world's leading superpower.

China sees a growing convergence of US, Japan, and Bharat interests in countervailing the former's rise. A resurgent Bharat and Japan's increased military activism are perceived as a threat by China to its regional predominance, and it looks at employing intimidating force as a way out for neutralising the informal alliance.

Under the aggressive leadership of Xi Jinping, China has unilaterally extended the maritime boundary in SCS, by staking claims to island territories of ASEAN nations, constructing and fortifying artificial islands in disputed waters, and arbitrarily establishing the 'Nine-dash Line' to assert its control over the maritime region. This has enabled it to advance its EEZ and consequent right to exploit natural resources in the region, simultaneously also strengthening its maritime defence. China today has more than 40% share of the world ship manufacturing industry, which has enabled it to put to sea a navy exceeding US Navy in terms of ship numbers. Geostrategically China is now able to hold its ground against the US-led freedom of navigation operations (FONOPS) in SCS maritime region.

On the economic front Xi Jinping has rolled out two strategic programs, the 'Made in China 2025' to overtake US leadership in key new age technology sectors of the economy, and 'China Standards 2035'by which China seeks to proactively standardise international technology and trade guidelines to facilitate its economic domination. The Digital & Space Silk Road under its BRI is designed to achieve the Chinese objective by 2025.

China's Roadmap for a New World Order

Development of Comprehensive National Power (CNP)

China is pursuing its world vision with single minded vigour by developing unchallengeable CNP through two robust parallel strategies. The first is by expanding the hard power of its armed forces to be the dominant strategic force. The second route is by developing an overarching economic strength. (11)

Expanding Hard Power

China's quest for world dominance has led it to develop the third largest nuclear stockpile. The Peoples Liberation Army Navy (PLAN) has overtaken the US Navy in terms of the number of ships and is now the largest ocean going navy. The Shanghai Security Cooperation Organisation (SSCO) is being used by China as an instrument to project influence in the Central Asian region, with an eye on securing energy supplies for her ever-expanding economy. Leaving aside South Korea, Japan, and Bharat, all other neighbours of China have fallen under its sphere of influence, with varying degrees of subservience to Chinese interests. ASEAN and other countries in the region, right up to Australia, are sensitive to Chinese interests.

China is determined to prevent the establishment of any rival centre of power in the region. Taiwan and Japan to its east, India to its west, and ASEAN countries to its south are all under intense Chinese pressure through the intimidating deployment of its armed forces. China is now confident of its overwhelming armed might and is leaving no opportunity to signal to the world its willingness to use force to enforce its Sino-centric global vision.

Economic Power

China is advancing its economic power through multiple initiatives under the BRI umbrella by establishing a lead in strategic new age technologies, investment in strategic infrastructure projects and key industries, offering secured commercial loans, and acquiring influence in key international agencies and countries to manipulate favourable policies. (12)

It has developed a huge trade surplus against the majority of large economies and is already the second largest economy in the world. It continues to be one of the most dynamic and fastest growing economies and is projected to cross the US economy in GDP terms by 2040.

China is promoting Regional Comprehensive Economic Partnership (RCEP), a free trade agreement which has been signed in November 2020 by countries that include South Korea, Japan, Australia, New Zealand, and ten of the fifteen ASEAN countries. RCEP is poised to emerge as the largest trading bloc in the world and truly showcases China's dominance as an economic powerhouse. It is crafted to be a key vehicle to expand Chinese economic influence by enmeshing the regional economies of South East Asia with its own domestic economy.

BRI – Surface, Digital and Space Silk Roads

China's most ambitious policy initiative for world dominance is aimed at restructuring and dominating the world of finance, trade, industry, and geopolitics by developing and employing new-age disruptive technologies. 'Made in China 2025' strategy envisages China to be the world leader in cutting edge technologies of Quantum Computing, Blockchain, Artificial Intelligence (AI), 5G, Internet of Things (IoT), Global Positioning Navigation and Timing (PNT), Space based Voice and Data Network, Remote Sensing and other Space based services. The BRI, projected to boost overall global trade by up to 6.2% and its regional corridor economies up to 9.7%, aims at developing China as the world's foremost economic powerhouse. The sheer scale of the envisaged technological lead will enable China to reap geopolitical dividend by reshaping the global power architecture to its advantage.

The BRI was initially conceived by China in 2013 for developing regional surface communication infrastructure, linking regional markets across continents, to promote economic cooperation. The development projects would stimulate economic growth in the region with the capital being provided as secured loans, from within China's capital reserves built up through trade surpluses. The goods and services too would be provided by China's manufacturing industry which had a surplus production capacity.

By 2016 the BRI was expanded to include integration of regional markets through the latest technology digital space, and space-based infrastructure and services, 'The Digital and Space Silk Road'. The capital for executing the infrastructure development work is being routed through financial and banking institutions setup and controlled by China, such as New Development Bank and Asian Infrastructure Investment Bank. The strategy is aimed at establishing a new economic world order, as an alternative to the existing international structure controlled and regulated by the Western economies. It would, in the long run, also translate into a geopolitical world responsive to China's interests.

To advance China's stranglehold over the creation of the alternate global infrastructure, China is providing silent state support through capital and technology infusion to setup global corporations, such as Huawei, Alibaba, Tencent, ZTE etc. Undercutting and outbidding rivals through price manipulations, enhancing scale and speed of operations, and acquiring controlling stakes in identified global technology companies are the route being followed by Chinese corporations to marginalise competitors.

Security loopholes embedded in software and hardware, locating data servers and data storage in Chinese-controlled space would enable China to access data to pursue its national interests. China's control over major flow of digital data, the world over, will assist it to gain dominance in research and development of emerging technologies, outmanoeuvre competitors, and influence state policies, enabling it to reshape world economic and political architecture to its advantage. Lack of adequate manpower to operate the technologically advanced digital infrastructure is inducing the underdeveloped countries to outsource operations to Chinese organisations, thus providing it additional data access.

The impact of the economic ascendancy of China through its Digital Silk Road initiative can be assessed from the estimation that development in the IoT alone could add upto US Dollar 1.8 trillion in cumulative GDP for China by 2030. 5G is estimated to generate US Dollar 975 billion of economic output, while the Next Generation AI Development Plan projects to generate US Dollar 21.6 billion demand in new sectors of the economy in the country by 2030.

China's digital products and services share of the global e-commerce market has already gone upto 42%, and it is among the top three in the world for venture capital investment in key types of digital technology, including virtual reality (VR), autonomous vehicles, 3-D printing, robotics, drones, and AI. China also has plans to upgrade its national telecommunications system to 5G, with an investment of US Dollar 411 billion. It has also begun implementing a plan to become a cashless society by introducing crypto RMB currency.

But the program with the most far reaching implications to sustain its lead into the future is the deep space exploration plan. The plan envisages not only wealth generation through economic exploitation of deep space but also as a means to sustain its global technological lead and superpower status. Technological advancements leading to the domination of space will also enable the domination of Earth.

The first stage of the plan, the BeiDou navigational system, a 35-satellite system for providing a global network for positioning, navigation, and timing services, is functional and shall be the key to all spheres of the BRI project. It will provide commercial services in the fields of communication, hydrological monitoring, weather forecasting, geographic information, time synchronization for communication systems, power dispatching, emergency response, public security, and several other fields.

China is already following through the second stage of its space expansion plan with the launch in 2018 of the first of the Hongyan constellation of 320 low-orbit satellites slated to provide a global two-way, real-time data transmission system along with other multimedia data services. It is intended to replace the existing ground-based communication networks, allowing uninterrupted global communication, and constant global coverage of all air, shipping, and overland routes, providing China with the winning edge in both the economic and geostrategic arena.

China's AI-assisted Quantum Computing will enable it to conduct real time predictive analysis of the phenomenal amount of data it will be able to access through its worldwide spread of data networks and space sensing assets. It needs no gainsaying that China's dominance in digital space, coupled with its technological advancement in AI assisted surveillance & analysis, data harnessing, computing, and predictive analysis would also provide it with winning edge in future military conflicts.(13)

China undoubtedly has a well charted roadmap to coerce the world to kowtow to it.

Influencing World Opinion

To understand the importance attached to the psychological warfare domain by the Chinese leadership one must delve deep into their culture.

Both Chess and the Chinese game of Weiqi are board games that are played by employing abstract strategy. Weiqi is a game of encirclement in which securing the positional advantage is the key. Chess on the other hand focuses on destroying the opposing pieces. The cognizant will talk about this subtle nuance between abstract strategy employed in the two board games, to comprehend the psyche of the Chinese and grasp the concept of the strategy employed by them to achieve a specific aim. To them, the Chinese strategy is premised on gaining psychological ascendancy over the mind of the opponent by inducing the latter to think the Chinese to be invincible.

The Chinese military thought propounded by their famous strategists is all about indirect battle. Giving way when the enemy is strong and taking recourse to offence when the enemy is weak. To win the war without fighting is to them the acme of military leadership. Hence psychological warfare to instil shock and awe on the minds of the opponent and sap their will to fight is a key strategy for the Chinese.

China has combined its Information Warfare and its Psychological Warfare wings into a joint Directorate to seamlessly conceive and launch long-term operations to support its strategic aim of world domination.

The mainline of Chinese propaganda projects an awe-inspiring image of an undefeatable China, which can be opposed only at great risk of economic reprisals which may have an adverse impact on such country's common citizens. To attain its end goals, it covertly promotes organisations and individuals amenable to tow China's national interests in the domestic governance space of their own country. These organisations and individuals assist in deep manipulation of the public opinion to influence their government's attempts, if any, to undertake coercive action against China. (14)

Nations inimical to its interests are having a democratic form of government. China subtly influences electoral outcomes in key democratic countries through electoral donations and paid media news with the aim to attempt at a formation of Government that is sensitive to China's interests. (15)

China also actively pursues proxy investments in influential media organisations of influential countries, donations, and paid news space to manipulate media reports. (15)

Modus Operandi

China has been engaging in acquiring financial stakes in holding companies of influential foreign media through direct investments, paid advertisements, donations, and outright purchase of news space in print and visual media. (16)

It is also alleged to have been involved in acts to compromise some key functionaries of institutions in which it has an interest, through a combination of multifarious inducements and outright coercion. (14)

China also allegedly takes recourse to covertly creating a supportive environment in rival countries by funding individuals and organisations amenable to its control. In other words, establish favourable 'persons of influence'. (14)

It is equally subtly influencing key appointments in International Agencies, such as UNO, WHO, IMF etc to toe the Chinese line. Compromised key top functionaries are used to make comments favouring the Chinese agenda, against target countries. (17)

It also subtly influences electoral outcomes in the interested countries through electoral donations, use of social media and paid media articles. (14) Fake social media handles are created to manipulate opinion favourable to the Chinese viewpoint.

PART II

The Present

> The Dragon's quest for destiny,
> leads it to rarefied heights,
> To the Wise One it was ordained,
> that the Dragon shall go astray.

Chapter IV

The 2020 Bharat China Standoff

The sting of the scorpion lies in the tail.

Multiple Chinese Incursions and Riposte By Bharat

Patience is a virtue whose strength is more than neutralised by the vice of greed.

Backdrop

It was the year 2017 and China was engaged in its road infrastructure development activity in disputed territory adjacent to Doklam in Sikkim close to the sensitive Bharat-Bhutan-Tibet tri-junction. Bharat for the first time decided to forcefully challenge the 'normal' nibbling territorial encroachment policy of the Chinese by employing troops to stop the road construction. This led to a two and half months 'battle of nerves' between the two countries. China was surprised by the unexpectedly firm resolve and military response of Bharat. The standoff between the troops of the two countries ended with China deciding to back off, clearly unprepared and unnerved by the forceful action of Bharat. It was a big setback to the carefully cultivated 'Wolf Warrior' image of the Chinese armed forces and resulted in tremendous loss of face domestically and internationally. China's psychological ascendancy of more than half a century over the Indian state had been lost.

Pursuant to this major policy change, Bharat also began speeding up its own logistics and communication infrastructure along the northern borders with Tibet. The newfound confidence of Bharat rang alarm bells in Beijing, as it sensed a threat to its critical alternate land access to the Indian Ocean and energy centres of West and Central Asia.

By mid-2019, Bharat had revoked the special status of J&K, under Article 370 and Article 35A of its constitution, followed by reiterating its resolve to regain POJK and Chinese occupied Aksai Chin and Shaksgam Valley regions of J&K.

Voicing open opposition in diplomatic forums to the BRI initiative designed to further the geostrategic interests of China, cultivating close bilateral ties with Vietnam for commercial exploitation of natural resources in SCS disputed by China, actively engaging with the as yet informal 'Quad Alliance' partner countries, and developing close military co-operation with the USA, were actions of Bharat which China interpreted as threatening its regional supremacy and critical national interests.

Bharat was emerging as a regional challenger to China's supremacy in Asia and a stumbling block to China's ambitions of global pre-eminence.

The pivot to the east by the US challenged Chinese dominance in SCS maritime region and fuelled growing independence leanings in Taiwan and ASEAN countries. The commencement of rearmament by Japan signalled its re-emergence from self-imposed geostrategic restraints and the rise of another challenger to established regional supremacy of China.

China perceived growing encirclement by emerging inimical geopolitical alliances. It also felt emboldened by its superior CNP, based on the visible strength of its economy and its modern and strong armed forces. Faced with a growing two-front threat that could impede its world vision, China chose to exercise the option of an overwhelming show of force, short of an open conflict, to overawe its opponents into submission. With decisive USA presence in the eastern maritime region, Bharat in its perception was the weaker opponent to intimidate through a show of force.

Relative Force Levels
China

The complete IB/LAC with Bharat is the operational responsibility of the Western Theatre Command of China. The Theatre Command has full command and control over all the Field formations and Military Districts in its area of responsibility.

The field forces available to the Theatre Command are grouped in three Army Groups, equivalent to Corps size formations, with reserve formations directly under command of the Theatre Headquarters.

Fighting field formations on its military order of battle (ORBAT) comprise 1 x Armoured Division, 1 x Mechanised Division, 3 x Motorised Divisions, and 3 x Infantry Divisions, overall, 8 Divisions. It also holds 2 x Armoured Brigades, 2 x Mechanised Brigades, 2 x Motorised Brigades, and 2 x Infantry Brigades, a total of eight additional Brigades.

It has one Mechanised Infantry Division stationed at Hotan closer to Laddakh, one Mechanised Infantry Brigade and two Mountain Infantry Brigades located in Eastern Tibet closer to Arunachal Pradesh. Other formations, including supporting arms and services formations, are located far in depth.

The PLAAF resources are also directly under the Theatre Command. In addition, an Airborne Brigade is also available for vertical envelopment tasks.

Bharat

In contrast, Bharat has three Army Commands, Northern Command, Central Command and Eastern Command, responsible for the IB/LAC with China. Their fighting field formations are grouped in four Corps with eight Infantry/ Mountain Divisions, two plus Armoured Brigades, and two Infantry Brigades deployed in the near vicinity of the operational areas. Two additional Corps size field force, with four Infantry Divisions, and an additional Infantry Division have also been allotted and are now being reorganised to bolster the offensive defence capabilities along the LAC.

The Air Force assets, however, are not allocated to the Commands and are employed centrally in close coordination with the Army. The Army Headquarter reserve Parachute Brigade is also available for contingency tasks.

The Indo Tibetan Border Police, under Ministry of Home Affairs (MHA), is responsible for manning the IB/ LAC during peace. It is placed under the operational control of the Command Headquarters only during war. Assam Rifles, a paramilitary force, is also responsible for manning the IB/LAC during peace. It is under the operational control of Command Headquarters.

Review

Relative to the deployable field forces along the borders, there is near parity in the opposing land armies. But the high-altitude warfare battle experience of the Bharat Army gives it an operational edge over the PLA Ground Force, as evidenced at Galwan river valley and Kailash range operations. The Bharat Air Force holds a thin qualitative edge over the PLAAF owing to effective high-altitude operational experience, superior support infrastructure and technical parameters enjoined by high altitude related factors. The Bharat Navy also holds an operational edge over the PLAN due to extensive operational experience, regular interoperability exercises with foreign navies, home base advantage in area of likely maritime operations and domination over critical maritime choke points.

Senior Military Leadership of China Tasked for Operations against Bharat

General Zhao Zongqi was the Commander and General Wu Shezhou the Political Commissar of Western Theatre Command, responsible for military operations along the land borders with Bharat.

General Zhao Zongqi, the Commander Western Theatre Command, had served 20 years in the Tibet Military Command, **commanded the Chinese troops during the Doklam incident** and was in line for promotion to CMC, the highest Military body of the Chinese Armed

Forces. In December 2020 he has been replaced with General Zhang Xudong.

Lieutenant General XuQiling assumed the command of Western Theatre Command Ground Force on promotion to the rank of Lieutenant General, in end April 2020.

Lieutenant General Wang Haijiang took over the responsibility of the Tibet Military Region. He had been erstwhile Deputy Commander of the South Xinjiang Military District which exercises frontline responsibility and jurisdiction over the Hotan and Ngari Military Sub-Districts. Eastern Laddakh frontier comes under the Hotan Military Sub District.

Major General Liu Lin, who had been serving with Headquarter South Xinjiang Military District since 2015, was promoted as its Commander in 2019. He also headed the Chinese military delegation at Chushul/Moldo for talks with Lieutenant General Harinder Singh, Commander of Leh-based XIV Corps of Bharat.

Three of these Generals were delegates at the 13th National People's Congress. All the Generals involved in the Laddakh Standoff were either die hard loyalists **of General Zhao Zongqi**, or had been serving for years on the border with Bharat. Political loyalty and professional competency may not always be synonymous.

Conduct of Military Operations by China

Pursuant to existing border management protocols between Bharat and China, there is an extensive No Man's Land ranging upto 20 kilometres from the IB/LAC, and is dominated by frequent patrolling by either side in disputed areas. Both the countries differ in their perception of the LAC. Regular army is not deployed along the IB/LAC. ITBP and Assam Rifles are deployed to patrol the Bharat side of the extensive no-man's-land. Patrolling on the Tibet side is performed by the Border Guards, under their Military Districts. The use of firearms is prohibited under the border management protocols, though carriage of personal weapons is optional by the patrols. Protocols also lay down extensive drills to avoid physical contact between the border patrols.

By February 2020 the COVID-19 virus outbreak, originating from the Wuhan laboratory in China had assumed a global pandemic dimension resulting in the largest lockdown in the history of mankind.

Traditionally both Bharat and China conduct annual operational training by their frontline field formations along the LAC during summer months. Owing to the impact of the COVID-19 virus, Bharat cancelled the operational training scheduled for the summer of 2020. China, on the other hand, continued to go ahead with the planned operational training of its field formations.

China assembled its offensive field formations in operational areas, in beginning of May 2020, under the garb of training movement, and launched simultaneous incursions along the entire length of the LAC from Depsang Plains, Galwan river valley, Hot Springs, and Pangong Tso in Laddakh to Naku La in North Sikkim.

In well planned trans-LAC military operations, China tasked its border troops for intruding into and establishing defensive positions in disputed areas in Galwan river valley, Hot Springs and Patrolling Point 4 at Pangong Tso.

It followed up with the overt deployment of one reserve Mechanised Infantry Division in the general area of Depsang Plains to support the operations at Galwan river valley. The deployment also threatened the sensitive Indian defensive position of DBO that dominates the approaches from Karakoram Pass to Nubra river valley, in the depth of Siachen Glacier. It also has a strategic advanced landing ground that can be used for dominating China's strategic surface communication infrastructure in the region. Bharat had recently completed the construction of a strategic road along the Shyok river to DBO. This road passes along the confluence of Galwan and Shyok rivers.

Another reserve Mechanised Infantry Division was deployed in depth of Pangong Tso to support the operations at PP 4 along its northern bank. Spanggur Gap and Rechin La across the Kailash range lie in close vicinity to the south bank of Pagong Tso. The two passes permit easy access for mechanised formations to cross Kailash range to threaten Chushul advanced landing ground and defensive positions guarding approaches to sensitive depth areas. It was an overwhelming show of force to deter Bharat from any retaliatory action.

The operations progressed as planned by China. Galwan river valley was occupied, exposing the road along Shyok river to DBO. PP 4 was also occupied along the northern bank of Pangong Tso. The national leadership of Bharat was stunned into inaction, surprised by the extent of military incursions and the force levels deployed by China.

The initial response of Bharat followed the traditional official stance of denial and obfuscating the situation. However, as so often happens in the fog of war, the unpredictable stubborn reaction of troops on the ground can at times carry the day even against overwhelming odds and change defeat into victory.

The daylight killing, by employing spiked batons and stones, of the unarmed Commanding Officer of 6 BIHAR of Bharat at Galwan valley by Chinese troops proved to be one such psychological turning point. Burning with rage at the gruesome killing of their unarmed Commanding Officer the soldiers of 6 BIHAR, though heavily outnumbered, rallied around their junior leaders and on the spur of the moment charged ferociously into the new Chinese positions. This impassioned action by 'the mad breed of ordinary men' put the cat amongst the pigeons at Galwan, usurped the Chinese victory, and scripted a change in the destiny of Bharat with their blood.

20 soldiers of Bharat were killed in this action. Chinese troops suffered an estimated 40 to 100 fatal casualties. Most surprisingly, during this entire action not a single bullet was fired! The psychological impact on the hierarchy of China of the disastrous execution of this operation can be gauged from the fact that it took them more than eight months from the action, to accept only four fatal casualties.

The commercially available real time satellite imagery and social media activism brought the incident into the public domain, inflaming passions within Bharat. China, while analysing the likely course of action that Bharat may adopt, had failed to take into consideration the power of social media activism of the young and vibrant Bharat, home to the largest middle class in the world! Bharat too had miscalculated the impact of this factor while adopting the traditional response of denial and obfuscating the situation. The 'nationalist' and people savvy political leadership of Bharat was quick to sense the change and ordered their armed forces to counter the Chinese deployments by use of force, if necessary.

Analysis of Chinese Incursions

Geostrategically speaking, the Chinese military operations were intended to proactively coerce and dissuade the emergence of any block inimical to its strategic interests, by reasserting China's dominance not only on Bharat but in South East Asia at large. It also intended to showcase the determination of China to safeguard its national interests, to the international community at large and its near neighbourhood specifically.

Domestically, there was rising internal discontent against CCP because of COVID-19 pandemic induced economic slowdown. Achieving military success against Bharat would draw attention away from economic and social discontent within China.

Successful operations would also impede infrastructure development work being undertaken by Bharat along the IB/LAC.

The incursion plan was craftily designed to outwardly conform to their policy of creeping annexation to achieve initial operational surprise. Simultaneously fifth columnists were employed within Bharat to domestically push for retaliation and use the retaliation as the raison d'être to inflict a swift and sharp bloody nose.

Incursions were simultaneous and spread over a vast frontage from Laddakh in north to Sikkim in north-east, to overawe and psychologically coerce Indian leadership to succumb to Chinese pressure. The surprise, speed and follow up operations involving the full spectrum of Chinese state agencies, indicate protracted planning and rehearsals over an extended period of time, and point towards orchestration of these military operations at the highest levels within China.

Geostrategically the situation was inimical to Chinese interests to launch major incursions at a juncture when it was already under extreme international pressure due to blame for COVID-19 pandemic, investigation of role of WHO in assisting cover up by China, ongoing US FONOPS in SCS maritime region, formulation of an alliance of like-minded powerful international countries against China, and increased scrutiny of its human rights violations in Xinjiang, Tibet and Hong Kong. The **launching of such an operation at a geostrategically inopportune time could not have been undertaken by Western Theatre Command without a go ahead from National leadership.**

The area for land annexation operations was carefully selected. The Galwan river valley, flanking Depsang Plains, and Fingers 4 to 8 along Pangong Tso was chosen for launching military incursions. The terrain in these general areas has narrow valleys with steep gradients, which preclude bypassing operations at a tactical level, thereby providing tactical and strategic advantage to their forces. The area was also critical enough to invite an aggressive Indian response.

Overwhelming local numerical superiority was ensured during operations in both sectors by an overt build-up of additional frontline field formations to support the incursions.

Subterfuge and deception were well planned to deflect blame and achieve surprise, despite formation level build-up.

A coordinated psychological warfare campaign was simultaneously launched and executed by all state agencies, including diplomatic channels. Incursions were extensively covered in the Chinese state and social media to showcase PLA as an overwhelmingly superior force. Fifth Columnists were also activated within Bharat, as part of psychological warfare campaign, to sow internal discord, swamp resources of security agencies, divert government attention and slow down state response.

Riposte by Bharat (18)

After protracted military level talks to resolve the issue, China initially agreed to pull back its forces, then procrastinated, and finally withdrew partially in Galwan river valley. It refused to pull back its troops from the northern bank of Pangong Tso.

Spanggur Gap and Rechin La, to its East, provide an easy approach to Chinese mechanised forces and infantry to threaten Chushul and to turn the flanks of Bharat's forward deployments in the region. Magar Hill, Gorkha Hill and

Gurung Hill along the Kailash range dominate the Spanggur Gap and also provide observation over Moldo base of the Chinese Army and their strategic road communication network in depth.

Black Top, Helmet and adjoining heights on the south bank of Pangong Tso are of tactical importance. They dominate Chushul plains and provide ground observation of Sirijap base of China and general area Fingers 4 to 8 lying on north bank of Pangong Tso and Chinese troop concentration in their depth areas.

Technical surveillance by Bharat began detecting increased infantry and mechanised forces concentrations of the Chinese Army in forward areas of the south bank of Pangong Tso and the vital Spanggur Gap, in mid-August 2020. Bharat assessed an imminent threat to Chushul airfield and forward deployments of its forces in the region. On night 29/30 August 2020 Bharat launched a pre-emptive three-pronged operation along the north and south banks of Pangong Tso and heights dominating Spanggur Gap and Rechin La.

The operation was spearheaded by 7 VIKAS, a unit of Special Frontier Force (SFF), closely supported by other infantry and mechanised forces. In a night-long operation, Bharat secured ridgelines along the north bank of Pangong Tso, overlooking Finger 4, recently occupied by the Chinese Army in violation of standing border management agreements between the two countries.

The second prong of the operation by Bharat secured Black Top, Helmet, and adjoining heights of tactical importance to the south of Pangong Tso.

The third prong secured Magar Hill and Gurung Hill, which dominate the Spanggur Gap, and other tactical heights dominating Rechin La.

Analysis of Operations by Bharat

These operations herald the emergence of Bharat from sixty years of psychological dominance of China, and finally laying to rest the ghost of the 1962 debacle. For the first time, Bharat has orchestrated its own incremental annexation military operations, mirroring Chinese policy, and succeeded in stymieing China.

The strategically important Chushul advanced landing ground had become dormant owing to Chinese domination post-1962 war debacle. With the commanding heights under own control, Bharat has opened up the option to reactivate the dormant Chushul advanced landing ground, further enhancing its operational capabilities in the region.

The SFF rank and file generally reflect dual loyalties – loyalty to Bharat, their foster country, and to The Dalai Lama. The Dalai Lama stood for peaceful resolution of forceful occupation of Tibet by China. This played a major role in hesitation on the part of Bharat to employ the SFF in open conflict against China. The publicised employment of SFF troops to launch offensive actions against China signals the handing over of reins by The Dalai Lama to the next generation Tibetan-in-Exile leadership, who are comfortable with the use of force to free Tibet from Chinese occupation. It also indicates towards the intent of Bharat to swing the international focus of the conflict horizon from Bharat-China confrontation to the Chinese occupation of Tibet.

But an even more important outcome for Bharat is the emergence of national leadership that is comfortable with a strong military and proactively dynamic in geopolitical affairs.

China has been shocked into military inaction as its military vulnerabilities lie exposed, shifting the focus from 'border management' to 'border defence'.

Geopolitically, China is suddenly at its weakest point in recent history, forced to confront the US-led alliance assembled in SCS and ECS maritime region to the East, while a resurgent Bharat holds China in a deadly embrace to the south-west. China is in a geostrategic trap of its own making, and this will lend further impetus and credence to actions to formalise the Quad Alliance.

Overall, China's propaganda induced myth of being a world power capable of challenging US dominance lies exposed. The Chinese leadership is finally the victim of the success of its own propaganda leading them to strategic overreach. Its inability to swiftly react to the changed operational outcome indicates faulty assessment and planning, and equally faulty execution.

The events are yet to run the full course, but the writing is there on the wall for all to see.

It is an unmitigated fiasco for China. The war aims of the Chinese military operations lie shattered on the rock and shale bed of Galwan river valley. The aura of invincibility so assiduously cultivated over decades by the Chinese propaganda machine has been broken. Despite having all the advantages of adequate planning, rehearsals, timing and terrain of own choosing, local superiority of numbers, surprise and deception, the best that China could throw at Bharat lost the plan. This dramatically highlights the fatal flaw of the Chinese system of political supremacy over the armed forces.

Future Geostrategic Course for Bharat

> *"You have not explored the frontiers of your*
> *full potential if you have not been called*
> *Mad at least once in your life."*

Bharat the New India

A new Bharat has emerged to the fore, replacing the pushover India of old. It is young, it is vibrant, it is proud of its legacy of yore and it is very-very expressive. It is this Bharat that is the driving force in the policy change, both within and without.

This new Bharat has already forced a changed outlook towards Pakistan by calling the bluff of the 'Mad Generals' of Pakistan who are ever ready to unleash unconventional weapons at the drop of a hat. This outlook has been replaced by the new 'narrative' of 'Businessmen Generals' of Pakistan running paranoid from an unpredictable Bharat which has seized the driving seat.

In just over two weeks at Galwan, Bharat has now shattered the carefully cultivated and hyped 'Wolf Warrior' image of China, forcing them to change the central theme of their psychological operations.

The young and vibrant Bharat is enamoured with the 'mad breed of ordinary men' of its Armed Forces who are the harbingers of this change.

Two Front War, a Threat to Bharat or a Dilemma for China?

When analysing the combat potential of adversaries, the number of feet on the ground and the guns seldom give the true picture. While the quality of the weapon matters, the hand behind the weapon and the leadership do play a defining role in the outcome of a battle.

Having lost the combat, both on the ground and in the perception of the world, China was at a loss. The death of large numbers of its soldiers may have been an inconsequential factor for a totalitarian regime, but the loss of its unbeatable 'wolf warrior' image so assiduously created over a protracted period of time, was vital to their goal of attaining superpower status without having to fight a decisive war.

The realisation has dawned on the leadership of China that it cannot win a war against Bharat on the battlefield. This has forced China into a mid-course policy correction to its erstwhile information warfare strategy which projected China as the land of unbeatable 'Wolf Warriors' to the new strategy of posing a two-front war threat, in conjunction with Pakistan, against Bharat.

The Reluctant Allies

Pakistan is precariously poised with a dominant India to its east, exposed western borders with Iran and Afghanistan, growing internal fissiparous tendencies in Baluchistan and Sindh, an unstable economy, an ill-equipped armed force, and an acute shortage of war fighting stocks.

Even more critical is the suddenly opaque geopolitical waters posing the distinct possibility of cancellation of massive outstanding loans, an economic disaster in the making. The Pakistan Army General Staff, the decision makers for their nation, understand Pakistan's vulnerability in the geopolitical space in entering an open conflict as an ally of China against Bharat.

Pakistan Army and their leading Generals preside over a business empire worth US Dollar 20 billion or even more. In an open conflict this business empire can well become a lucrative target.

China has invested US Dollar 20 billion worth in infrastructure projects within Bharat's strategic reach. A shocking realisation has also dawned of Bharat being capable of carrying the battle to the Chinese eastern coastline, to even Beijing, and playing havoc with their merchant shipping.

The Revised Chinese Information War Strategy

The revised Chinese two front war threats to Bharat is being projected by stressing the deployment of two Chinese mobile divisions deployed at Depsang Plateau and eastern Laddakh with additional mobile field formations in depth, up scaling of Chinese air assets in Tibet, and reported sightings of Chinese air force assets in POJK.

The commitment of Pakistan to the new strategy is being depicted through deployment of its two Infantry divisions in the Gilgit – Baltistan area opposite Laddakh, and activation of Pakistan Air Defence radars along the LC.

The desired aim is to weaken Bharat's will to fight by unnerving its leadership and creating public apprehensions on its preparedness to withstand two front war with China-Pakistan.

The Counter Theme of Bharat

Bharat too is rolling out a subtle and yet menacing psychological operations strategy, hitherto a forte of China, to unnerve Beijing.

The Chinese messaging is crude, shrill, and lacking the subtlety associated with a cool and well-crafted strategy by an inscrutable China. It reflects the nervousness of Rawalpindi and the uncharacteristic lack of self-confidence in Beijing.

Pakistan's showcased deployments are defensive in nature and more in the form of an insurance against a surprise strike from an unpredictable Bharat. Pakistan has left itself an escape clause.

Quiet movement of mountain strike formations of Bharat from peacetime locations to its northern borders, signal its will to fight it out. Also, the representatives of Bharat at Army level talks have stiffened their stance to reiterate its strong resolve to resist China.

Pivot by three US aircraft carrier groups in open seas adjacent to Taiwan and the SCS, move of US Stryker

Brigades, Marines and Air assets to South East Asia, reported deployments of Japanese and Australian naval assets near the SCS, joint naval exercises by the informal Quad Alliance countries, statements of unequivocal support to Bharat by powerful world leaders, are being projected to trap China in a two-front war.

Policy Dilemma Before China

China's revised information warfare strategy has strong chinks.

Pakistan lacks offensive capabilities in the mountains and its air defence environment is weak. The strong possibility of Pakistan collapsing under the weight of internal contradictions and external geopolitical pressures could at one stroke permanently jeopardise China's strategic investments and vital national interest of an alternative land access to the Indian Ocean.

Centrifugal forces in Xinjiang and Tibet are in check only due to a strong Chinese military presence. The prolonged deployment of its troops opposite Laddakh could adversely impact its internal security situation, which may lead to a domino effect in other sensitive regions.

China has already lost face in South East Asia, emboldening ASEAN countries and the Philippines to start voicing opposition to unilateral Chinese actions in the region. A major reverse or even a stalemate may create an adverse impact on its painstakingly built maritime security infrastructure in SCS.

A menacing partnership is taking shape along the eastern maritime region of China, threatening its maritime trade lifeline. The US has interposed itself strongly in contested waters to the east of China. Japanese rearmament is nearing completion and Australia is modernising its security infrastructure. Myanmar, the Philippines, and ASEAN countries have openly opposed Chinese unilateral actions in SCS.

Major Chinese investments in infrastructure projects in Africa are under threat of nationalisation.

Tibetan Government-in-Exile, Uighur minorities in Xinjiang, Hong Kong, and Taiwan are again gaining centre stage in key international forums.

Trade and economic sanctions are adversely impacting the Chinese economy. The spectre of civil unrest could potentially threaten the very roots of CCP hegemony.

The geostrategic environment has become too uncertain for China to simultaneously focus on its exposed eastern coastline, south-western borders with Bharat, internal security situation in Xinjiang and Tibet, and manage the deteriorating economic situation.

Military Sphere

Air

Substantial deployment of Chinese air assets in POJK is potentially a double-edged weapon. Firstly, it provides Bharat 'casus bellicus' to launch proactive air operations, critical for it to secure the vital edge. Secondly, it advantages Bharat to gain local air superiority by employing concentrated air assets against spatially divided opponents.

The terrain favours Bharat for air operations. Its air assets are well poised, being on internal lines of communication, to optimise employment against both adversaries, without major shifting of base.

The weak air defence environment in Pakistan exposes all military assets and logistics infrastructure within its land space to destruction from air. There is nothing China can do to improve this situation.

The numeral edge of the two adversaries is considerably neutralised by the quality of Bharat's air assets, its superior sortie per aircraft ratio, its superior combat support infrastructure and **readily available reliable external support.**

Naval

The much hyped Chinese maritime 'String of Pearls' has more to do in gaining propaganda traction during peacetime. During open hostilities, they are indefensible and are of value only for hunkering down its merchant shipping and naval assets which are vulnerable on the high seas.

Bharat has both the will and capabilities to neutralise them in pre-emptive naval operations. Operational support from countries with mutual interests will further enhance its maritime domination in the Indian Ocean region and bottling up the Malacca Straits.

China and Pakistan both lack a true blue water navy to enforce FONOPS in hostile maritime waters. Inability to ensure freedom of navigation for their own merchant shipping implies a break in their maritime trade, severely impacting their economy.

Bharat on the other hand has the option of clubbing its merchant shipping operations with joint FONOPS under the security of naval resources of countries with mutual interest.

Major naval losses by China in naval confrontation and/or disruption of its maritime trade will destabilise her economy, generate internal fissiparous tendencies, and embolden the South East Asian countries to reinforce their maritime claims to the disadvantage of China.

Land

China lacks **deployable** land combat resources to ensure a decisive outcome along the LAC. Bharat does have adequate resources to secure limited gains in certain sectors and achieve an overall stalemate.

Decisive support from Pakistan too is not available as it lacks major offensive capabilities in the mountains. In the plains, the battle-hardened mechanised strike formations of Bharat are more than capable of carrying the battle deep into Pakistan.

But what should be of major concern to China and Pakistan is the capability with Bharat to inflict prohibitive destruction on their logistics and economic infrastructure along CPEC, and also sever their surface communication network link.

New-Age-Warfare

Bharat has already achieved mutually assured destruction parity with China in space assets.

The invisible war for dominance in the information and cyberspace domain is already actively underway.

China's strategic road map for world domination through the 'Digital Silk Road' is being disrupted and is under sustained diplomatic attack by Bharat in conjunction with the US.

As with BRI, Bharat has taken the lead by blocking Chinese social media apps and Information Technology companies engaged in Chinese 'Digital Silk Road' infrastructure.

A Geostrategic Trap Awaits China

Ominous military build-up by countries inimical to its interests, in the maritime region off China's 14000 kilometres long eastern coastline, is already underway. The country which swears by Sun Tzu's 'Art of War', willingly falling into a geostrategic trap, by actively engaging militarily with Bharat at a time when the stronger enemy is knocking on its main door, may well prove to be its biggest humiliation.

Review of Options for Bharat

Erstwhile India's diffident and reactive approach to Chinese designs was highly reassuring to the latter. It enabled China to engage India at ground and time of its own choosing. The timid Indian policy to suppress information on border incursions by China is no longer feasible in today's age of commercial availability of real time satellite imagery and social media activism, and shall be counterproductive in the long run.

There is consensus in the strategic community that the only way to dissuade China is dialogue from a position of strength and willingness to employ force. With its logistics infrastructure and force deployments in place, Bharat needs to adopt a proactive stance to impose caution on future Chinese actions. The ideal course would be to keep China unbalanced by signalling a determination to mirror the Chinese policy of incremental territorial encroachments.

The process of setting up its own Theatre Commands needs to be speeded up by Bharat. The current command and control organisation is too tedious and time consuming for a swift operational riposte.

Military Options

Be prepared for localised skirmish by employing Special Forces and force multipliers.

Proactive deployment of Combat Groups/Integrated Battle Groups.

Showcase resolve to target Chinese economic assets in POJK. The existing ground situation and rules of open engagement across the LC in POJK legitimises such engagements.

Plan for maritime blockade at choke points, as a last resort.

Geostrategic Options

Encourage legitimacy to Taiwan in international fora, in conjunction with other major allied countries.

Work towards penalising China for 'Human Rights' abuse and genocide in Tibet, Xinjiang, and Hong Kong by applying international economic sanctions, in conjunction with countries with similar interests.

Enhance indirect support to Tibetan Government-in-exile in voicing their concerns.

The Chinese government is equally adept at sending and reading geopolitical signalling. Once Bharat signals its intent through **actions,** China will receive the message. Strong political leadership backed by actions of a strong military are a prerequisite for adopting this course of action.

Future Geostrategic Course for Bharat

The focus has now shifted from 'border management' to 'border defence', a prolonged and costly option for both countries. The mutual distrust of intentions is unlikely to bring a quick resolution to the conflagration.

Bharat now needs to follow through by shifting the focus of talks between the two countries from 'defining of LAC' to 'defining the borders'.

China has violated all past agreements on conflict management along the LAC. It has also consistently refused to exchange maps. Hence Bharat is well within its sovereign rights to abrogate all erstwhile border/LAC agreements between the two countries. The LAC should be as per physical occupation on the ground.

Bharat also needs to stress upon China to desist from undertaking any activity in POJK and withdraw from Shaksgam valley illegally ceded by Pakistan to China.

China's refusal to accede should be taken as interference by China in Bharat's internal affairs. This will clear the way for Bharat to openly come out in support of a free Tibet.

The world cannot afford to undergo a catastrophe because of conflict between two nuclear-powered neighbours spiralling out of control. In any case, China's claim to Tibet is tenuous at best and is being enforced due to geopolitical might enjoyed by China currently. Tibet has never been the private property of any nation or leader to be gifted on a platter to appease China.

Historically, Tibet has been a free nation in its recorded history of more than two thousand years except for two short interludes in the 13th and 18th century CE. In fact, China has been under the reign of foreign dynasties for a greater period. Tibet, as we know today, was first unified in the Seventh century CE and was one of the most powerful Asian Empire till 10th century CE, also controlling the region of present-day Chinese provinces of Gansu and Yunnan. Tibet is also deemed by many to be the spiritual cradle of the world and legends abound of visits by great Saints of most major religions to this region.

National boundaries are being redrawn the world over and new nations emerging. Tibet too needs to be pulled out from the enforced grip of China and given its legitimate place in the comity of independent nations.

A free and independent Tibet as a buffer between Bharat and China appears as the ideal option for avoiding a future clash of two of the world's great civilisations.

The follow through on formalising of the Quad Alliance also requires to be fast paced.

Chapter V

Silver Warriors Perspective on Bharat

The Silver Warriors as Quintessence Bharat

Between us we represent the full spectrum of Bharat.

We were 238 on commencement of training, of which 213 were commissioned into our Armed Forces with a contractual obligation of 5+5 years of service, on a bright and sunny day in Officers Training Academy, Chennai then known as Madras. We represent almost all the states forming part of the Union of India and were commissioned into the complete spectrum of Regiments/Corps/ Arms of the Indian Army. Collectively we have served across the entire length and breadth of the country and participated in all the military operations of Bharat during our times.

Five years later, based on options exercised, 87 were absorbed permanently into the Army on being granted permanent commission. The balance 126 of us were released on completion of contractual service based on options exercised, over the next five years, and fanned out to be entrepreneurs in logistics/hospitality/aviation; self-employed professionals in education, legal and security domains; leaders in the public sector banks, RBI, Coal India, ASI; corporate in Infrastructure Development, Manufacturing, and Education sectors; and Civil Service/ Police/PMF cadres. But the bonds remain, even today.

More than forty years down the line we have 27 of our dearest in heavenly abode. Of the 186 survivors, we are 136 of us still banded together under the tagline 'Silver Warriors', an informal Strategic Group. We share our joys, sorrows, and our religious festivals. We debate our ideas of Bharat, and yes, we at times are acrimonious in our likes and dislikes, but we are one big extended happy family, stretching across the length and breadth of Bharat. Even as senior citizens we are ever ready and willing to take up cudgels on behalf of Bharat.

Like the weapon systems we have exploited to the fullest, our bodies too bear the dents and scars of full exploitation, externally and internally. Like the weapon systems we handled, we too are in the last quarter of our assessed shelf life. We love India for whom we have willingly shed our blood, and now we love Bharat even more, ever willing to take up cudgels for its defence. We may be physically somewhat frayed at the edges, but mentally we are still agile, robust, and passionate.

We have participated in all military operations by our armed forces for over three plus decades. As such we are aware of the full spectrum of military threats facing Bharat.

We have engaged in all counter-insurgency operations. Hence, we are aware of the nuances of internal threats to our motherland.

We have taken up issues with all the state governments on behalf of our Jawans. This has made us aware of the strengths and areas needing improvements in our provincial and local systems of governance.

We know our men like the back of our hand. This has enabled us to be aware of the social and religious fabric across Bharat.

We have provided 'Aid to Civil Authorities' across the length and breadth of the country. This has enriched us in knowing the skill sets of our governance structure.

We have been successful entrepreneurs. This has wizened us to the 'ease of doing business' in the country.

We have served in a wide spectrum of professions across the country and even abroad. This has enabled us to be aware of the nuances of corporate governance.

We have had deep interactions with political dignitaries, diplomats, and foreign armies. This has provided us insight into the world of geostrategic plays across the globe.

We have been actively associated with domains of research & development, deep state covert organisations, infrastructure development, logistics of scales, et al. Most probably if you speak of it, we would have done it!

Our collective and widely diversified professional experience, coupled with our geographical spread across Bharat enables us to know the pulse of the nation at any given point in time. We are qualified, we are experienced, and we are confident enough to share our vision of Bharat.

Silver Warriors Perception of Bharat

Bharat is not a nebulous term. It is enshrined in our constitution.

Our constitution names our country as '**Republic of India**' in English language version.

'***Bharat Ganarajya***' is how our country is named in the Hindi language rendering.

India is a name given to our land by foreigners. Bharat is our heritage bequeathed to us by our ancestors.

The emotional appeal of the ancient civilisation of Bharat on its present-day citizens and that intangible strength which has enabled it to outlast its enemies through thousands of years of turbulent history is best summed up in the extracts from '*Saare Jahaan se achha Hindustan hamara*' by Allama Mohammad Iqbal:-

> *"…Unan-o-Misr-o-Ruma sab mitgaye jahaan se,*
> *Ab tak magar hai baaqi naam-o-nishan hamara.*
> *Kuch baat hai ki hasti mitti nahi hamari,*
> *Sadiyon raha hai dushman daur-e-zaman hamara…"*

What poet Iqbal refers to in his famous lines quoted above, is true even today. We face powerful adversaries along our northern and western borders. It is the unparalleled bravery and professionalism of our armed forces that keeps them at bay. When the armed might of Bharat wavers, it is the nation that falters.

The intrinsic strength of Bharat lies in its thousands of years old cultural, scientific, social and religious heritage. The Bharat of our forefathers is an inclusive civilisation comprising of all philosophies, castes, creed, culture, and religion.

We specifically highlight the aspect of religion. History is witness to the fact that maximum blood has been shed, the world over, in the name of religion. Yet Bharat has been the birthplace of four major religions, Hinduism, Buddhism, Jainism, and Sikhism, and all these religions have been born in peace.

Bharat is the oldest civilisation the world has known, with the richest cultural and scientific heritage. Even today the world is struggling with scientific concepts which were part of our daily life thousands of years ago.

The scientific knowledge encoded in the ancient religious texts of Bharat is deemed to be myth, simply because the learned scientists and researchers of today are unable to perceive the vastness and complexities of the cosmos well known to ancient Bharat.

The holiest number for Bharat is 108. In **astronomy,** the **number 108** intriguingly connects the sun, moon, and earth: the diameter of the sun is **108** times that of the earth, and the distance between the sun and earth is approximately **108** times the diameter of the sun. Similarly, the diameter of the moon multiplied by **108** equals the distance between earth and moon.

As per modern science, the *Vimanas* of ancient Bharat fail to meet the scientific rigour to fly. But if the same modern principles of aeronautical science were to be applied to a bumblebee then it too should not be flying, but it does, and so did the *Vimanas* of ancient times. So advanced was our **aeronautical science**.

We are the only civilisation with a world view – '*Vasudev Kutumbakam*', the world is one.

Acquiring Knowledge ranked the highest in society. Accordingly, the Gurus were next only to Parents.

Our seats of learning at Nalanda, Taxila, and Sharda Peeth were without parallel in the world, and are the **forerunners of modern Universities**.

Knowledge was learned at *Gurukuls* and not taught by rote. Today we call it **experiential learning**.

All aspects of nature were worshipped. Today we call it **sustainable development**.

Giving alms to the needy, care for the infirm and aged, and piety was a way of life. Today we have to legislate **corporate social responsibility**.

We understood cosmic connectedness where each thing has a consciousness. Today we call it the **theory of black body radiation**.

We knew of the existence of the invisible matter. The invisible planets Rahu and Ketu are part of our astronomical and religious heritage. Today science calls invisible matter as **Dark Energy**.

We have gone beyond the conventional concept of time to comprehend the **cosmic scale of time,** where *Kaal* can imply both time and death, time is cyclic and not absolute, and that time has different dimensions at different cyclic levels.

We have gone beyond the conventional understanding of allopathic medical science to understand that **psychosomatic ailments** are a reality.

We understand how to utilise, through yoga and meditation, our cerebral mind to explore and tap the unknown **solar plexus consciousness** and the inexhaustible source of energy therein.

We seek to temper our materialistic yearnings with a **higher purpose of life** through the pursuit of *Dharma, Artha, Kama,* and *Moksha.*

It is Bharat that connects us to the part of our heritage that gives us access to ancient knowledge that modern science is just beginning to explore.

Yoga Sutras of Patanjali, containing the science of yoga and meditation.

Sushruta Samhita on knowledge of medicine derived from Atharva Veda.

Sthapatya Veda by Vishwakarma containing architectural and mechanical science secrets

Vishwakarma Vaastu Shastra, containing the secret to harnessing the flow of etheric and magnetic energy.

Vedanga Jyotish containing knowledge of astronomy.

Aryabhatiya on mathematics.

Kautilya ka Arthashastra, a treatise on statecraft.

Vedas, Upanishads, Puranas, Bhagavad Geeta, Ramayan, Mahabharat and innumerable other scriptures awash with cosmic knowledge.

All these scriptures predate any known parallel texts in any other ancient civilisation.

We have to connect to this Bharat of yore, which has done this in ages gone by and is a shining beacon of hope and strength in these factitious times.

Individually the best way to reconnect to the Bharat of our forefathers is by pursuing '**The Five Point Principles to Regenerate the Spirit of Bharat**':-

Actively seek **knowledge**.

Actively imbibe **green practices** in daily life.

Actively engage in **concern and care** for the disadvantaged section of society.

Actively work towards a **higher purpose** in life.

Actively work for the **integrity** of Bharat.

And we must never ever forget that it was our internal dissensions that enabled foreign rule and not because the invaders were stronger than us.

It is our bounden duty, as citizens of the great nation that we are, to pledge and ensure that we never let it happen again.

As a soldier, we understand that decline of Bharat commenced the day our factitious internal warring ensured decline of our CNP relative to our economic wealth.

Development of CNP must now be our single point agenda.

Silver Warrior's Vision for Bharat 2030 CE

Preamble

Seventy years post-independence we are still a deeply factitious nation. The political class to further their political interests of maximising votes to gain and retain power, has exacerbated and exploited every conceivable divisive grouping possible in society – religious, language, regional, social, ethnic, and cultural.

A largely corrupt political class, woeful standard of governance, costly and laborious process of judicial redress, antiquated education system, a weak law and order and governance machinery, have disincentivised individual pursuit of commerce and industry and given rise to a largely unscrupulous society.

Scant regard for environmental degradation and a high population growth rate is forcing unsustainable exploitation of natural resources. The biggest impact is likely to be felt on the availability of water and forest cover, critical for the survival of future generations.

A complete governance and social transformation are the need of the hour to avoid the breakup of the nation and ensuing blood bath.

This can only take place from the very top echelon of the Government and shall need to be pursued with vigour for the lifetime of a generation.

Principles of statecraft propounded in '*Arthashastra of Kautilya*' should form the basic tenet for transformation of the Bharat *rashtra*.

Transformation of Society

The society needs to be engaged at large to move towards **wilful compliance** of norms, and rules and regulations of the state.

Introduction of measures to wean the society away from corrupt practices through **universal enforcement** of laws.

Guarantee of **quality education** upto Middle school, to generate greater awareness of issues critical to the health of the society and the nation at large. The New Education Policy brought in by the Government is a much-needed step in the right direction.

Concept of '**One nation One Law**' needs to be implemented to marginalise divisive tendencies.

Terminate caste-based divisions in society and replace them with the **principle of economic security**. Principle of 'One family One Assured Job or Minimum Wages in lieu' through Direct Bank Transfer. Beneficiary voluntarily leaving a job, to be debarred from social benefits for a specified period.

Incentivising **voluntary control of the population** is a must to ensure balance in the exploitation of natural resources.

Political/Electoral/Parliamentary Transformation

We are realistic enough to understand that it would be an utopian idea to have our politicians, like our armed forces, embrace the principle of keeping national interest foremost in all their actions and dealings – '*Desh sarvopari lagan*'.

But we do envision our elected representatives in Parliament and State Legislatures to behave in a manner befitting the ideals of Bharat, in action and debates; parliamentarians that we as citizens are proud of. Disciplined elected representatives are a prerequisite to a disciplined citizenry. To ensure this aspect we propose

Suitable 'Rules of Conduct for Members of Parliament (MPs) and Members of Legislative Assemblies (MLAs)', with strictly enforceable penalties as for the Civil Services and Armed Forces.

Principles of mandatory presence of MPs/MLAs in Parliament/State Legislatures when convened and sitting, no work no pay, right of recall by the electorate, no criminal record, and only one pension, need to be enforced through law.

To safeguard against political party dictatorship, the elected representative should have the freedom to vote on Bills as per individual conscience; with the proviso of mandatory vote of confidence from the electorate, whenever (s)he votes against the respective party whip.

Political parties need to be compliant with their own party constitution. Ensuring compliance with this aspect should be included in the charter of The Election

Commission. All hearings of the Election Commission should be open to the public and record of minutes of its meetings made public.

The utilisation of public funds, other than as passed by the Parliament/State Legislature, should be punishable by law. The Office of Comptroller and Auditor General should be mandated to pinpoint responsibility for the purpose.

Transformation of Law & Order Machinery

Efficient Law & Order machinery is an essential ingredient for the social cohesion of a nation, which is vital for economic enterprise.

Ensure impartial and effective compliance to criminal rules and regulations by establishing Police Commission as an independent constitutional body with judicial powers over members of the police force.

Recruitment of psychologically profiled manpower for police force.

Police manpower should be specially trained for investigation by employing modern scientific investigative tools.

Streamline police working environment to bring in greater efficiency.

Enhanced police is to public ratio at par with more developed countries.

Deputation of Indian Police Service officers to Central Armed Police Forces should cease.

Judicial

Establish National Judicial Advisory Council as an independent constitutional body.

Establish fast track courts for minor and petty offences carrying a maximum sentence of one year and under and introduce automatic bail for non-cognisable offences. This will also bring down the jail occupancy.

Transformation of Revenue Administration

Revenue administration is one of the major fountain sources for the spread of corruption.

Revenue assessment should be made software centric to optimise collection of revenue and ensuring compliance to revenue and taxation laws.

Promote and incentivise e-governance.

Central Vigilance Commission and Central Information Commission be given Constitutional authority status with well-defined judicial powers of contempt for non-implementation of its orders.

Development of Comprehensive National Power

Major reforms in the organisation of the National Command Authority and National Security Council to align these organisations to proactively steer the nation to meet future full spectrum technological and physical threats.

Armed Forces

Restructuring of armed forces to optimise utilisation of combat resources and battle readiness to fight the invisible spectrum 3D WAR – Deniable Disruptive Destruction.

Development of capability for enhanced 'Out of Area Operations'.

Introduce changes in armed forces qualitative requirements for recruitment and training parameters, in tune with future conflict scenarios.

Research & Development

Enhanced investment in indigenous research, development and manufacturing of high technology defence weapons and equipment.

Initiate thirty years perspective plan for cutting edge frontier technology research in the teleportation of matter, hydrogen energy, warp drive propulsion, and exotic directed energy weapons.

Prioritise Indigenous Manufacturing

Self-sufficiency in high technology weapons and equipment.

Cyber Information Security

Evolve and invest in comprehensive national cyber information security infrastructure.

Economy & Commerce

Minimum Government control for setting up commerce ventures.

Introduce automated, time-bound Government clearances for ease of doing business.

Corporatise all Government commercial ventures.

The Labour reforms now introduced by the Government shall provide the right fillip to the manufacturing sector.

Banking

Promote digital market economy.

Environment

Forest Cover

Enhancement of green cover through sustainable afforestation, laying greater stress on maximising survival of planted saplings rather than on the quantity of saplings planted, and software-enabled ground and aerial surveillance.

Green practices

Encourage green practices through incentives.

Promote reusable items.

Green construction norms be made mandatory in the infrastructure sector.

Garbage segregation and collection.

Conservation

Promote conservation of natural resources, especially water.

Promote Environmental Awareness

Waste recycling.

Renewable Energy

Enhanced impetus to increase renewable energy power output.

Ten Critical Imperatives 2020 - 2030 CE

1. Legislation for **'voluntary control of population'**.

2. **'Principle of economic security'** based on 'One family One Assured Job or Minimum Wages in lieu' through Direct Bank Transfer.

3. **Legislation** to enforce mandatory presence of MPs/MLAs in **Parliament/State Legislatures** when convened and sitting, no work no pay, right of recall by the electorate, no criminal record, and only one pension.

4. Establish **Police Commission** as an independent constitutional body with judicial powers over members of all the state and central police forces.

5. Establish **National Judicial Advisory Council** as an independent constitutional body.

6. Promote and incentivise e-governance for greater efficiency and marginalise corrupt practices. Central Vigilance Commission and Central Information

Commission be given Constitutional authority status with judicial powers for well-defined contempt for non-implementation of its orders.

7.   **Restructuring of armed forces** to optimise utilisation of combat resources and battle-ready to fight the wars of the future.

8.   Evolve and invest in comprehensive national cyber information security infrastructure.

9.   Promote and incentivise the **digital economy**.

10. **Water conservation**.

PART III

The Future

"*Against the Chinese it is cheaper to be prepared for war than having to fight one.*"

Chapter VI

Peep Into the Future

The quest for dominance drives commerce, so to discern the future follow the trade. Harmonised growth of power and commerce presage stability, imbalance in the two shall portend strife.

Geostrategic Portends in Asia 2020-2025

(First published by Centre for Joint Warfare Studies, New Delhi in August 2020 and reproduced with their kind permission.)

"Rise of a challenger to an established regional or global power is invariably disruptive of geopolitical peace."

General

In the geostrategic circles, the 21st Century is already being talked of as the Asian century, wherein the dynamics of forces being generated by the rivalry between US and China, and Bharat and China, on the other hand, will deeply influence the discourse of international relations the world over. Within Asia, the primary factor which is shaping the geostrategic alignments is the energy security needs of China.

For almost a decade one of the most anticipated event horizon in the geostrategic space has been the rise of China as a challenger to US supremacy in Asia and the world at large. History is a mute testament to any such climb of a challenger being disruptive to regional and world peace. China's upsurge is no different.

To the student of history, it is quite interesting to note great similarities in the ascent of China in Asia and the earlier disruptive rise of Nazi Germany in the 1930s in Europe. Quite like Nazi Germany, Communist China is seeking land and maritime space well beyond its borders, engaged in Human Rights abuses against its own minorities, employing armed might to impose its will on the weaker adversaries, actively violating well defined international conventions and agreements, and refusing to implement decisions of lawful international judicial organisations.

Even more interestingly, like Nazi Germany, Communist China is heavily dependent on imports for energy security, lacks maritime prowess to defend its maritime trade in hostile situations, and is engaged in the cardinal geostrategic sin of simultaneously opening all fronts against its adversaries.

But this is where the similarities end. Quite unlike Britain and France, the then Great Powers of Europe neighbouring Germany, Bharat has chosen to confront China along the mutual borders on the Himalayas and is willing to pursue the conflict into a full spectrum of modern war. This has taken China by surprise, habituated to a traditionally submissive response from erstwhile India to provocative actions by the former.

Similarly, unlike in the 1940s where the US entered the battlefield against Germany more than two years post commencement of World War II, the US has now taken ab initio lead to confront China in the SCS.

Chinese hierarchy is well known for its long-term policy focus. Hence its decision to open a second front to its south-west in the Himalayas, while still engaged in the east against aggressive US maritime posturing in SCS, has surprised the geostrategic community world over. To understand the constraints that are driving Chinese actions on a seemingly self-destructive course, we need to look at its geostrategic imperatives.

Imperatives of China

"Measures undertaken by a nation to overcome its strategic vulnerabilities are the most obvious targets for the opponent."

Critical Vulnerabilities

China has four critical vulnerabilities. Firstly, its political and economic core is most vulnerable to maritime threat along its exposed 14,500 kilometres long coastline. Secondly, its economy is critically dependent on energy imports. Thirdly, its access to open waters of the Pacific Ocean is confined by Japan to the east, while the restricted maritime region of Malacca Straits impedes its trade routes towards the open waters of the Indian Ocean. Fourthly, it lacks the naval capability to safeguard its maritime trade routes for ensuring uninterrupted energy supply during active hostilities.

The Chinese leadership is pragmatic enough to comprehend these vulnerabilities. Once we too appreciate these realisms, it is easy to comprehend the imperatives of China in embarking on the course of action it is undertaking.

Employing Remedial Measures

China is unlikely to possess adequate maritime capability to be able to secure its maritime trade routes, at least for the coming decade. Without an uninterrupted supply of energy resources the Chinese economy will collapse, setting in motion centrifugal forces leading to the collapse of the government itself.

Chinese actions in SCS are primarily focused on securing an extended defensive parameter that can inhibit the employment of offensive maritime force by its adversaries against its exposed coastline, thus enabling it to marshal its resources to the west to secure overland energy routes to West Asia and Central Asia.

Its establishment of 'String of Pearls' bases along its critical energy supply maritime trade routes is to be seen as a nascent attempt to impart some semblance of security to its maritime trade.

Its BRI should be looked at as an attempt to open up alternate energy supply lines. CPEC and CMEC are two critical components of this strategy. However, the threat from Bharat has put a question mark on the viability of these projects.

Another alternative is to expand its reach to overland energy routes into Central Asia and West Asia energy sources. It has already tapped Russia for energy supply through trans-Siberia energy pipelines. Another probability is to develop energy pipelines through Central Asian Republics or Wakhan Corridor of Afghanistan into oil rich regions of Central Asia, Iran, and Iraq.

It is this criticality of China that is making it the common thread running through the geostrategic realignments taking place across East Asia to West Asia.

Broad Realignments in Asia

"Between capability and intent of an adversary, it is realistic to keep an eye on its capability building. Intent is nebulous to discern and can change overnight, capability building takes time and is also easy to monitor."

The interplay of differing factors is influencing the changing geostrategic realignments in South-East Asia, South Asia, West Asia, and Central Asia.

In South-East Asia the challenge being posed by China to US supremacy is the key factor influencing the realignment of forces.

In South Asia, it is the animosity between Bharat and China that is shaping the alliances.

In West Asia the challenge being posed by Shia predominant Iran to the leadership of Sunni leadership of Saudi Arabia is the dominant force influencing regional dynamics, coupled with China's search for energy security.

The Sunni predominant Central Asian Republics, under the watchful eyes of Russia, are currently keeping aloof from the alliances taking shape in their neighbourhood.

China also looks at the Central Asian region as the panacea for its energy needs.

With China and Iran on the brink of entering a major strategic partnership, the former becomes the common link in the realignment of geostrategic forces across the length and breadth of Asia. Thus, the realignments are broadly coalescing into pro and anti-China forces.

Active intervention by the US in all the affected regions of Asia has devolved the mantle of leadership of anti-China forces on the US.

Russia, heavily dependent on its energy resources for the strength of its economy, is currently non-committal, though keeping itself relevant by its intervention in Syria and supply of high technology military equipment to warring factions.

South-East Asia

The territories of Japan in conjunction with Taiwan and the Philippines control direct access of China to the open waters of the Pacific Ocean. Chinese control over Taiwan would enable the former to gain unhindered access to these open waters. On the other hand, an independent Taiwan, due to its proximity, poses a significant potential threat to the Chinese mainland.

China's unilateral use of force in SCS to establish its 'nine-dash line' has brought it into conflict with almost all major ASEAN bloc countries. Similarly, its threat to use force against Japan, Taiwan, and South Korea to resolve maritime and sovereignty disputes has pushed them to align against China.

Japan has already speeded up its rearmament and is determined to act as a bulwark between China and its unhindered access to the open waters of the Pacific Ocean. Propped up by US support, Taiwan and ASEAN are emboldened to voice open criticism of unilateral Chinese actions.

Most curious is the shift in the stance of Australia, from being deemed to be part of the Chinese sphere of influence to becoming its leading critic. China, by far the largest trading partner of Australia, had surreptitiously acquired controlling stakes in multifarious strategic industries and projects in the latter country and was even influencing the outcome of their democratic elections.

However, the unravelling of Chinese conspiracy to make Australia subservient to its interest has generated a backlash in Australia. The latter is now taking the international lead for holding China accountable for COVID-19 pandemic. Its newfound anti-China stance is also influencing Australia to lend physical support to US maritime deployments in SCS. Retaliatory trade action against Australia by China has only strengthened Australian resolve to pursue its anti-China stance.

The US has now deployed its naval armada to inhibit further expansion by China into the disputed maritime regions of South East Asia. It is also leading the efforts to form a broad coalition of Japan, Australia, the US, and Bharat to counter Chinese expansionist designs.

China is currently content with securing its gains in the SCS and to wait out the US naval task forces.

South Asia and Bharat-Chinese Adversarial Factor

The comprehensive victory by China over India during the 1962 war had resulted in a very long-lasting shock and awe impact on the decision makers in Delhi. This resulted in Chinese provocations along the Himalayan borders drawing predictably meek response by India, barring a few personality based aberrations by commanders on the spot.

However, India's transformation into a resurgent Bharat, during the Doklam incident of 2017, severely jolted China. It views this resurgent Bharat as a threat to its long-term energy security.

The geostrategic location and military potential of **Bharat** makes it a lynchpin in any strategy to choke energy routes of China. Along the Himalayas, the CPEC and the CMEC are both within the strategic interdiction capability of Bharat. Similarly, the maritime energy trade route of China can be choked from the maritime base of Bharat at the Andaman and Nicobar Islands.

The actions of Bharat to fast pace infrastructure development in Laddakh, enhancement of mountain specific deep interdiction combat power, publicly stated resolve to liberate the POJK and the Aksai Chin regions, increasingly close strategic alignment with the US, and active participation in the development of the US – Japan – Australia – Bharat Quad Alliance are causing deep concern to Beijing.

The decision by China to take coercive action, short of open hostilities, against a resurgent Bharat before it becomes too strong is predictable in view of China's propensity to threaten or employ force to resolve bilateral disputes affecting its core interests.

The pre-planned ingress by China across the LAC in mid-May 2020 met with an unexpected tough response from Bharat. This miscalculation by China is now proving to be highly costly for it to pursue its strategic interest by force. China is also stymied by Bharat showcasing its resolve to pursue the standoff, if needed, into a full spectrum open conflict.

A nuclear armed **Pakistan** has proclaimed geostrategic designs of controlling or at least being able to influence the ruling dispensation in Afghanistan to its west. To its east it aims at annexing J&K through indirect intervention. However, it lacks the requisite economic strength and combat power to achieve its geostrategic designs. This overreach has seriously debilitated its economy, which is now hostage to foreign loans and commercial agreements biased in favour of China. This has forced Pakistan into a strategic partnership with China which is dictated by the latter.

China, in conjunction with Pakistan, has now posed a threat in being of a two-front war on Bharat. Here Pakistan is in a bind. The emerging geopolitical alignments in West Asia and South East Asia are inimical to it engaging in an open conflict with Bharat. The likely international trade and economic sanctions will lead to its fiscal collapse.

China has also succeeded in drawing **Nepal** into its orbit of influence. This will adversely impact on Bharat's combat potential along the Himalayas and should be a matter of serious concern.

It provides a bridgehead to China over the Himalayas. It makes the Siliguri Corridor dangerously vulnerable to interdiction. But the most dangerous fallout for Bharat would be the question mark on continuing effectiveness of its highly trained mountain warfare adept Gorkha troops amounting to almost three divisions strength.

Myanmar, Bangladesh, Sri Lanka, and the Maldives are maintaining a neutral stance.

Changing Alignments in West Asia

The Sunni and Shia Muslim religious divide has emerged as the major factor in shaping regional alliances in West Asia.

Saudi Arabia, as the defacto leader of the Sunni Muslim predominant countries, has formed a broad coalition comprising United Arab Emirates, Bahrain, Morocco, Sudan, Jordan, Egypt, and Yemen. It has also influenced Pakistan, dependant on Saudi aid, into providing freelance combat support.

This alliance has active material support of the US and tacit support from Israel, a US ally.

Israel, the only non-Muslim country in the region, has the strongest regional military with geostrategic reach encompassing almost the whole of West Asia. Its policy of pro-active intervention to safeguard its geostrategic interests makes it a powerful influence in West Asia geopolitics. In end June 2020 it has reportedly conducted a covert strike by employing Air Force, Cyber and Special Forces assets, on Iranian nuclear weapon and uranium enrichment facilities.

Iran has emerged as the defacto leader of Shia Muslim dominated countries. Iraq, Lebanon, Syria, and Kuwait are part of this alliance. Iran also holds considerable sway over Shia Muslims in other Asian countries, enabling its influence well beyond its borders.

Russia is providing indirect military technological support and influence to the Iran-led coalition.

The US, on the other hand, is openly employing coercive force as well as wide ranging economic sanctions against Iran to detract the latter from its indirect strategic intervention against the Saudi Arabian alliance.

Strategic engagement with the US is currently the cornerstone of Bharat's strategy to effectively withstand the coercive policy of China, the primary adversary of both nations. Hence, Bharat cannot afford to go against the US interest of neutralising Iran. Under US pressure Bharat has ceased import of petroleum products from Iran.

This has influenced Iran to undertake its own strategic policy realignments, which are inimical to the interests of Bharat.

China, with an eye for meeting its own energy needs, has seized this opening to enter a strategic alliance with Iran. The alliance is vital to China to further diversify and secure its overland energy supply lines.

The emerging **geostrategic alignment between China, Pakistan, and Iran** has inherent fault lines. Sunni

Muslim predominant Afghanistan gets squeezed between Shia Muslim predominant Afghanistan and Sunni Muslim predominant Pakistan.

The Afghan state does not possess the necessary strategic resilience to withstand any major external intervention. Any collapse of the Afghan state will release destabilising forces in the entire neighbourhood, which in turn will invite extra-regional intervention. This will also lead to a conflict of interest between Iran and Pakistan.

As the geostrategic situation heats up, a more far-reaching impact will be on the continuation of Pakistan freelance support to the Saudi Arabian alliance and the threat of consequent cut off from economic aid by the latter.

Sunni Muslim predominant **Turkey**, a militarily powerful nation in West Asia, is reasserting its power by actively intervening in the Syrian conflict as well as in Libya. To buttress its leadership claims in the region, it has also joined hands with Iran to jointly combat the Kurdistan factor and challenge Saudi Arabia leadership of the Organisation of Islamic States. Similarly, it is making overtures in support of Pakistan to wean it away from the Saudi Arabia alliance.

Egypt, with French support, is emerging from its self-imposed isolation to challenge Turkish intervention in Libya.

But the most serious ethnic-religious fault lines in West Asia today are in Iraq and the adjacent regions to its north, bordering Iran, Turkey, and Syria. 60% of Iraqis are Shia Arabs, predominantly concentrated in south-eastern Iraq bordering Iran, 20% are Sunni Arabs generally in western Iraq bordering Syria, and 17% are Sunni Kurds in north-eastern Iraq bordering Iran and Turkey. Approximately 25 to 30 million Sunni Kurds are the majority inhabitants of the border regions of Turkey, Syria, Iraq, and Iran.

Iraqi Sunni Muslim separatism and cross border **Kurdish nationalism** are highly potent movements readily available for exploitation.

This is the region that shall next fall prey to geostrategic machinations between the two opposing power blocs to tie down respective opponents.

Central Asia

An overwhelming 99% population of Sunni Muslims, numbering around 103 million, reside in Kazakhstan, Kyrgyzstan, Tajikistan, Turkmenistan, Uzbekistan, Afghanistan, and Eastern Xinjiang.

Shia Muslim Azeris comprise roughly 85,000 in Kazakhstan, 35,000 in Uzbekistan, 33,000 in Turkmenistan and 18,000 in Kyrgyzstan. 1.5 lakh Ironis, Shia Muslims of Iranian descent, inhabit Uzbekistan. Small numbers of Ismaili Shias inhabit Tajikistan.

85% of Afghans are Sunni Muslims, numbering around 33 million. Around 6 million are Shia Muslims, with another 4 lakhs Hazara Shia Muslims and around one lakh Buddhists.

The presence of Shia Muslims of Iranian descent provides Iran with a modicum of influence in Uzbekistan.

Central Asian Republics continue to remain under a strong sphere of Russian influence. Any attempts by them that go against Russian interests are likely to invite direct or indirect destabilising Russian intervention.

Russia is also wary of a strong and unchecked China neighbouring its thinly populated but mineral-rich eastern borders, especially as China also voices claim to the Vladivostok region of Russia.

Yet Russia has vested interest in tacitly supporting China. The latter is Russia's biggest trading partner, and geopolitically, deployment of US resources to confront China provides Russia greater room for manoeuvre to secure its national interests in Central Asia and West Asia.

Asia Portends for 2020-2025

'Essaying the excuse of 'stab in the back' is the strongest indication of incompetency in geopolitics and military affairs and should logically invite immediate sacking!'

The outcome of two events by November 2020 shall dictate the geostrategic course of Asia for the next five years.

First is the survival or downfall of Xi Jinping as China's President for Life, General Secretary of Communist Party of China and Chairman of Central Military Commission of China. The survival of Xi Jinping beyond November 2020 will be the clearest indicator of China continuing to march on the confrontationist course set by him.

The other is the victory or defeat of US President Donald Trump in his Presidential bid for the second consecutive term in November 2020. His victory will signal the continuance of US policy to aggressively challenge China in its backyard of SCS. On the other hand, the defeat of the incumbent President will entail a lame duck Presidency till January 2021, followed by another 2 to 3 months of settling down period of the new administration.

The latter course of event would likely provide a window of opportunity of four to six months to China to aggressively push forward with its geostrategic designs without encountering a cohesive challenge from the US. In this scenario, a strong possibility exists of China launching a short and sharp offensive, in conjunction with Pakistan, against Bharat. Hence late 2020 and early 2021 will be a decisive period. Depending on geopolitical alignments, with the Himalayan passes closed, it will also be an opportune moment for Bharat to launch pre-emptive military operations against Pakistan.

Likely Course of Action by China

The most critical factor for China during this period shall be the **security of its energy routes**, as it lacks the military potential to ensure the security of its maritime trade.

The CPEC and the CMEC are still under development and also vulnerable to interdiction by Bharat.

Central Asian Republic countries are highly volatile and not secure for routing energy supplies.

China cannot be solely dependent on Russian energy supplies through Siberia for strategic reasons.

That leaves it with the only viable alternative of diversifying energy supplies through the Wakhan corridor of Afghanistan to Iran.

Hence it is likely to **avoid prolonged open hostilities** and concentrate its resources to secure and **diversify overland energy routes to West Asia and Central Asia**.

China has been able to establish an extended defensive parameter in the SCS region to safeguard its vulnerabilities along the Eastern coastline. It is **unlikely to undertake any further provocative operations in the SCS region**, so as to ease pressure from the US and its allies. Under extreme pressure, it may even temporarily offer to enter negotiations to resolve disputes.

That will enable China to concentrate its resources to its west, on evolving security of its overland energy routes. Towards that end, its **primary focus shall be to neutralise Bharat**. China shall apply concerted pressure on Bharat through all available means at its disposal, including a short and sharp open conflict, if geostrategic opportunity favours this option.

Alliance with Iran and Pakistan is vital to China's energy security. However, because of inherent internal contradictions, China will be forced to divert major attention and resources to maintain the effectiveness of this alliance.

Neutralising Pakistan, the weakest link of this alliance, should therefore be the primary focus for the opposing coalition.

Options for the US

On the military front US is most likely to exert pressure on China and its allies along four points.

Indo-Pacific Theatre Command shall **continue to conduct FONOPS** in SCS and ECS, in conjunction with the nascent Quad Alliance and other friendly powers to exert pressure on China. US deployment will also provide a security umbrella to Taiwan, Japan, and ASEAN countries against any further maritime threat from China.

US Central Theatre Command shall adopt **offensive posture against Iran along Makran coast**, as also maintain over watch to ensure open access to merchant shipping in the narrow Strait of Hormuz.

The US will **provide strong material and diplomatic support to Bharat** for any military eventualities against China and Pakistan.

The US is also likely to **facilitate Sunni Muslim – Kurd coalition** in northern and western Iraq to apply further pressure on Iran and also tie down Turkey.

On the economic front the US will further expand the scope of **economic and trade sanctions against China, Iran, and Pakistan.**

The US will also **pursue Chinese human rights abuses** in international forums and provide **tacit support to efforts by Taiwan and Tibetan Government-in-exile** to achieve greater legitimacy as a sovereign entity.

Russia

Continued strife in West Asia is advantageous to Russian interests. It disrupts the West Asia energy supply, provides a market for its armament industry, and keeps the religious fundamentalist forces at a safe distance from its borders. Hence, Russia shall **continue with its presence in Syria**.

Russia also looks at Shia Muslim predominant Iran as a bulwark against Sunni Muslim supremacy in West Asia. The latter eventuality would boost fundamentalist forces in Central Asian Republics along its southern borders. Hence Russia shall continue to **provide tacit material support to Iran**.

A militarily dominant China is inimical to Russian interest. Despite extensive trade relations with China, Russia is **unlikely to back any Chinese actions against Bharat. It is also unlikely to overtly support China in its confrontation with the US**, Japan, Taiwan, and ASEAN in the SCS region.

Turkey

Turkey is a militarily powerful state, currently seeking to chart an independent course in the region. Its military intervention in Libya has brought it dangerously close to confrontation with Egypt and France.

Coupled with the increasing possibility of a resurrected Kurd separatist movement gaining tract in its south-eastern region, **Turkey will not have adequate resources at hand to effectively intervene in the unfolding West Asia imbroglio**.

Saudi Arabia led Coalition

This coalition will continue to engage in a proxy conflict with Iran led Shia alliance in Arabian Peninsula countries and in Iraq.

Israel

A deepening Iran-China strategic relationship will be a cause of most serious concern for Israel. Knowing China's propensity for nuclear proliferation, it could speed up the acquisition of nuclear weapons by Iran. Hence, Israel shall oppose this alliance with all possible resources at its command. Towards this end, its collaboration with Bharat will further deepen.

Iran

Iran shall deepen its **strategic partnership with China and Pakistan**. A flare up of Sunni separatism and Kurd nationalism in Iraq and the collapse of Afghanistan into warlordism will be of serious concern to Iran and will severely restrict its ability to pursue its interests in Syria and Lebanon.

Leveraging its Chabahar port sea access to landlocked Afghanistan, Iran shall attempt to extend its influence in southern Afghanistan. This shall be a potential flashpoint in its strategic relationship with Pakistan.

Pakistan

The deteriorating economic situation within Pakistan shall be a key factor in its facing internal centrifugal forces.

With a weakened economy, it lacks resources to combat separatist forces in its south, an unstable Afghanistan to its west, and increased pressure from Bharat to its east. Its economy is already hostage to heavy loans from multilateral international funding agencies. In the altered geopolitical alignments, the threat in being of withdrawal of these loans will be the most critical factor in determining its future course of action.

Pakistan's economy will be unable to withstand the fiscal shock of an open conflagration with Bharat and has no choice but to **avoid open hostilities with Bharat,** pressure from China notwithstanding.

Afghanistan

Unless the US reverses its decision to withdraw from Afghanistan, the latter will collapse to the dynamics of the China-Iran-Pakistan alliance. Mercurial warlords shall again dominate the country.

An unstable Afghanistan traditionally gives rise to fundamentalist forces. It will be a matter of great concern to the Pakistan-Iran-China axis and will force their physical intervention. This in itself will invite interference from not only Russia but the US and Bharat as well.

Japan

A rearmed Japan, rife with nationalist spirit, shall continue to defy Chinese attempts at intimidation and in conjunction with the US will be a threat in being to Chinese maritime trade.

Japan shall also deepen its economic ties with Bharat to enable the latter to pose a greater geostrategic challenge to China from the rear.

Taiwan

Taiwan, with strong US support, shall continue to chart a geostrategic course that will be inimical to Chinese interests.

ASEAN

Vietnam, Malaysia, the Philippines, and Brunei are ASEAN member countries directly impacted by Chinese unilateral action in claiming and enforcing its control over disputed maritime areas of SCS. Bolstered by US naval presence, the ASEAN grouping has voiced its concern over unilateral Chinese actions in the dispute.

This has provided US diplomatic support for its maritime deployment in SCS, as also assured logistics support bases in the region in the Philippines and Vietnam.

Australia

After unearthing the malicious undercover effort of China to undermine its sovereignty, containing Chinese expansionist designs and belligerence shall be the cornerstone of Australian diplomacy. It shall seek stronger alignment with the US, Japan, and Bharat to thwart China.

NATO

The deepening of the economic crisis in the European Union and reduction in US Armed Forces deployment from Europe restricts the scope of NATO engaging in major intervention in the Asia-Pacific region.

Limited military support from France and UK shall however be available to US in West Asia and South East Asia regions.

Way Forward for Bharat

"The best way out for Bharat to avoid a war with China is to actively prepare to fight the war. It will also be cheaper in the long run."

General

The rivalry between Bharat and China shall be long drawn out and will be played out across the full spectrum of conflict scenarios. Bharat has faltered in early discerning of the intent of China. There is no other way to explain the military predicament it faces of a two-front war from China and Pakistan.

Bharat shall now have to develop a two-pronged strategy to safeguard its interests. The first shall be to focus on urgent actions to withstand the joint threat in the immediate future. Second shall be the strategy for long-term impact.

Short-Term

The best option for Bharat is to proactively **secure a strong international alliance** in its support, to deter any open conflict by its opponents.

Thereafter, at an opportune moment, launch **swift pre-emptive naval and airstrikes against Pakistan**, the weaker opponent, to degrade its combat potential as also the surface infrastructure critical to the CPEC and other Chinese commercial and strategic assets in POJK.

This will provide Bharat breathing space to withstand pressure from China. Longer the wait, greater shall be the vulnerability.

Degrading Pakistan combat potential shall also adversely impact its direct intervention potential in Afghanistan.

Bharat will have to cater for a **prolonged dissuasive ground deployment along the northern borders.** To keep China unbalanced, the best course would be to mimic its incremental encroachment policy.

Naval deployment shall have to be affected such that it's a threat in being to choke Malacca Straits to Chinese merchant shipping. This will impose added caution on China for any attempts to pose an active ground threat along the Himalayas.

Bharat just cannot afford to let China call the shots in **Nepal and needs to take proactive steps to resolve the situation in its favour**. A strife torn Nepal is preferable to a Nepal acting at the behest of China. The situation has to be resolved with finesse and ruthlessness.

Priority shall have to be allotted to force multipliers, electronic and cyberspace warfare assets for urgent replenishment along with war fighting equipment, munitions, and supplies.

Long-Term

The integrity and independence of a **friendly Afghanistan has to be ensured through the pursuit of active geostrategic alliances**. This will divert valuable resources of China and its allies and shall assist Bharat to manage an overall favourable geostrategic environment.

An **independent Tibet** as a buffer between Bharat and China is in the best interest to maintain long-term peace and tranquillity across the Himalayas. This should be the long-term geopolitical focus for Bharat.

A well laid out diplomatic strategy needs to be executed to further own geopolitical interests with neighbouring countries.

Concerted drive by counterintelligence agencies needs to be orchestrated to **uncover and weed out Chinese fifth columnists** within the country. Lessons from Australian and Italian experience should be incorporated into own counter efforts.

The proposed reorganisation of Theatre Commands needs to be processed on priority. **Northern Theatre Command should extend from Pir Panjal in J&K to the border with Myanmar,** so as to effectively counter Chinese Western Theatre Command operations in POJK and Shaksgam valley.

The **Mountain Strike Corps** in its present organisation is unwieldy to be employed in the assigned role in the mountains. It needs to be **downsized into multiple, highly versatile, and mountain mobile Battle Groups.**

Vertical intervention, Special Forces, and long-range precision targeting capabilities need to be continuously strengthened.

Cyberspace being an invisible spectrum of war shall be highly vulnerable even during no-war no-peace scenario. There is a definite requirement to fast track cyberspace warfare capabilities.

National Security Council should be reorganised to integrate invisible spectrum warfare expertise.

The **Intelligence** acquisition, evaluation and dissemination setup has not been able to establish its efficacy, despite numerous recommendations for its streamlining. The Defence Intelligence Agency needs to be tasked and equipped to meet its own external intelligence inputs.

Peacetime **border management**, especially along northern borders, requires to be streamlined. All deployments of PMF/CAPF need to be brought under operation control of Theatre Commands.

Make in Bharat policy for defence equipment has to be given priority. The only cost-effective way to combat prolonged Chinese belligerence is through self-sufficiency in defence equipment.

(Col RS Sidhu, Sena Medal is a post graduate in History from Delhi University. He has authored various articles published in reputed service and think tank journals.)

Food for Thought

*The battle of Chanakya and Confucius has been joined
and the King shall lose no time for action.*

Restructuring Defence Architecture of Bharat

Apex Security Structure

Bharat is on the cusp of the most comprehensive reforms ever to its security infrastructure. The creation of the appointment of CDS and the amalgamation of the armed forces into the governance structure of the country through the newly established DMA are just the opening gambit in the changes envisaged in the country's defence architecture and its war fighting doctrine.

A sense of earnestness has been imparted by tasking of the CDS to roll out the reforms within his tenure of three years. The standoff with China and the posing of the threat of a joint two-front war by China-Pakistan adds further urgency to the subject.

The standoff with China has already snowballed into the most extensive threat being faced by India in the 21st Century. The physical standoff between the opposing forces along the Tibetan border is now acting as the proverbial smokescreen, camouflaging the ongoing full-fledged invisible spectrum 3D – Deniable Disruptive & Destructive – WAR being engaged between the two Asian giants. The outbreak of COVID-19 pandemic in conjunction with armed ingress on the borders, enhanced cyberspace attacks targeting critical assets of sensitive national installations and major Indian corporations, orchestrated fly by night public space vandalism, grey origin psychological warfare media op-eds propagating Chinese interests, are all 'Battle Indicators' of the ongoing hidden spectrum warfare between the two countries.

Evidently, the faceoff with China along the borders is also impacting the internal security dimension within Bharat in cyberspace, commerce, economic, political, and civil society domains. Evolving technologies in cyberspace, AI, biological vectors and unmanned air-land-sea mobile platforms are also introducing the external security challenges into the domain of internal security as well. This is redefining the concept of full-spectrum conflict, enabling nation states to engage in geostrategic rivalries by degrading the CNP of target nations without engaging in debilitating open warfare. Peacetime targeting of cyberspace, economic, commerce, and human capital resources is the new normal in geostrategic rivalry.

This overlap in external and internal security domains is generating ever complex scenarios necessitating a cohesive response from external and internal security apparatus.

Bharat has traditionally followed watertight domains while handling national security, with the MoD responsible for external security, and the MHA handling internal security. The Cabinet Committee for Security (CCS) is the apex decision making body for security affairs, with the National Security Advisor (NSA) as the advisor. A National Security Council (NSC) under the NSA, comprising of domain experts from key Ministries and key organisations, functions as an advisory body on security. The three service chiefs and now the CDS are conspicuously relegated as 'observers' in the key decision-making process.

In practice, however, there is minimal cohesion between external and internal security verticals. Kargil 1999, Pathankot airfield terror attack 2016, Doklam 2017, Galwan river valley 2020 are major red flags pointing to lack of effective co-ordination between the external and internal security organisations. Also, generally, the disputed borders should be under the purview of the armed forces, but the ITBP deployed along the contested border with Tibet is not under their operational control.

This necessitates a fresh look at reorganising the apex security structure. The NSC needs to be realigned to proactively steer the nation to meet the full spectrum of new-age threats. A super arching Ministry of Security or broad basing the NSC from an advisory to an executive role needs to be considered.

War Gaming New Scenarios

The extension of deep Chinese influence in Nepal is adding new external threat dimensions. The factitious internal politics within Nepal opens up an alarming scenario of Chinese military presence across the Himalayas in Nepal. Such a probability, no matter judged as howsoever improbable at the present juncture, will present an existential threat to the integrity of Bharat. Remember Tibet.

In a similar vein, **in roads by the Chinese and Pakistan establishments into the Bharat polity** have aggravated the internal security dimension within the country. Every pursuit of national development agenda is under challenge, posing the greatest dilemma for the internal security establishment. The government of the day is at its wit's end to counter it.

Restructuring of Armed Forces
Battle Ready for Wars of the Future

Fast paced advanced technological changes are presenting dynamic opportunities to innovate new concepts for applying in future battlefields. Paradigm shifts have already taken place from the hitherto fore three-dimensional land, sea and air warfare to **five-dimensional warfare** that includes space and cyberspace dimensions as well.

Technology is also shrinking the world enhancing the strategic reach of the armed forces. This is throwing newer **challenges in the field of communications and logistics infrastructure management.**

There is a new technological race on to develop and harness new sources of unconventional energy and **directed energy weapons**. The low visible spectrum firing signatures, very high velocity and lethal accuracy of these platforms has enhanced kill ratio while impacting the efficacy of active defensive measures.

Space-based surveillance, communications, command & control, and weapon systems have augmented battlefield transparency, reduced response time and increased response reliability. **Targeting and safeguarding the space assets** have introduced a new spectrum of warfare.

Synthesis of the triad of nanotechnology-based robotics, information technology and biotechnology is breaching the barriers in future frontier technology research, development of Quantum Computing and **AI weapon platforms**. Lethal swarms of self-propelled, AI enabled nano platforms and robotic soldiers are already being experimentally deployed on battlefields, revolutionising unconventional and Special Forces operations. The drone and missile strikes on Aramco oil production facility in Saudi Arabia, Nagorno – Karabakh war, and employment of drones by Pakistan to support its trans-border covert operations are visible indicators.

This will necessitate the armed forces to **invest in technologically savvy manpower**, fielding cyber and space warfare capable state of the art equipment, with enhanced communications infrastructure, furthering its strategic reach to defend core national interests.

The complexity of these specialised resources, their paucity, and the need for their seamless integration will be feasible only through **network centric command and control structures** down to the sub-units of the field forces to synergise their impact. The reformed defence architecture of Bharat must satisfy the criteria of agility, survivability, swift decision-response matrix, and effectiveness in the futuristic battlefield scenario.

Reorganising Northern Theatre Command to Combat Threat from China

Two dilemmas pose themselves when considering the restructuring of the existing four Command Headquarters responsible to safeguard the northern borders against China. The Government Order detailing the tasking of CDS and the three services headquarters does not encompass operational command of field forces. The Theatre Commanders shall report directly to the Government. Secondly, the unique geographical configuration of the northern land borders may make it too unwieldy to be managed by a single theatre command.

However there exists a strong case to not only have a single theatre command to counter the China threat, but also extend its geographical boundaries to include the LC with POJK upto the Pir Panjal range. It is of interest to note that Western Theatre Command of China has operational jurisdiction for the entire border with Myanmar, Bhutan, Nepal, Bharat, POJK, Afghanistan, and Central Asian countries bordering China.

Due to the existing complicity between China and Pakistan, any action by Bharat to recover POJK from Pakistan will impact Chinese economic and strategic assets and may lead to Chinese military intervention. Being the more powerful of the two, **POJK should be prudently evaluated in conjunction with a threat from China.** In any case, China has enmeshed itself as a party to the POJK dispute.

The core of China and its economically vital eastern coastlands shall not be within striking reach of conventional assets likely to be available to the proposed theatre command (s). This would be detrimental to the proposed theatre command (s) being able to adopt a credible dissuasive posture against China. To pose a credible threat the **theatre**

command (s) should possess requisite conventional military resources and have physical proximity to threaten the CPEC and the CMEC, the two economic corridors vital to China. This would impact the core interests of China. Multiple theatre commands to combat China will impact the development of cohesive operations. (19)

Extending the Northern Theatre Command boundary from Talu Pass in Arunachal Pradesh in the East to Pir Panjal, included, in the West would lead to multiple advantages.

It will provide flexibility in developing complementary operations against China on either flank.

The similarity of terrain along the theatre command frontage will generate economy of effort in optimum exploitation of combat resources.

Pir Panjal, a major land barrier, precludes credible Pakistan threat from south of Pir Panjal along inter-theatre boundary.

It would enable a calibrated response and pose a credible threat, from within integral conventional resources, to the core interests of China in POJK and Myanmar.

An overview of China's Theatre Commands is provided below.

Overview of China's Theatre Commands

The defence of China is organised around five Theatre Commands.

Central Theatre Command is responsible for the defence of the political core of China, including its seat of power, Beijing.

The **Eastern** Theatre Command is responsible for the defence of its economic corridor lying along its exposed coastline opening into the East China Sea and for power projection in this maritime region.

The **Southern** Theatre Command is responsible for the defence of its highly vulnerable southern coastal region and power projection into its most factitious maritime region, the SCS.

The **Northern** Theatre Command is responsible for providing depth to its political core from the north and power projection in the northern areas and Yellow Sea maritime region.

The Western Theatre Command is responsible for the protection of the CPEC and the CMEC, power projection towards Bharat and Central Asia, and assist the civil administration in quelling civil unrest in Xinjiang-Uighur, and Tibet Autonomous Region.

Jurisdiction of China's Western Theatre Command includes Sichuan, Tibet, Gansu, Ningxia, Qinghai, Xinjiang, and Chongqing regions. Geographically it is the largest of the five Chinese Theatre Commands.

Along borders with Bharat, the Western Theatre Command has under it the Xinjiang Military Command and Tibet Military Command. The former handles the border with Bharat in the Laddakh region. The Tibet Military Command handles border with Bharat, in Sikkim, and Arunachal Pradesh, and also with Bhutan.

The territories with a very high percentage of minority population in China are designated as **Autonomous**

Regions, a euphemism for annexed territories. China has 5 autonomous regions – Guangxi, Inner Mongolia, Ningxia, Tibet, and Xinjiang. Three of these autonomous regions, namely Tibet, Xinjiang, and Ningxia are with Western Theatre Command. This indicates a heavy focus on earmarking resources for maintaining internal stability.

Reorientation of Formations for Mountains

Even during the days of erstwhile India's Pakistan centric organisation of field forces one of the more interesting lacuna lay in the visualised tasking evidenced from the structuring of the offensive role formations. Internationally, retaining territorial gains across recognised IB are difficult to maintain and we never possessed the diplomatic capital to enable it. On the other hand, both Pakistan and erstwhile India did retain their trans-LC territorial gains during the 1971 war. Erstwhile Indian enclave of Chhamb across Munnawar Tawi river is now under Pakistan control.

But erstwhile India unexplainably maintained three Corps size mobile strike formations for employment in the plains along the IB, with no specialised corps size strike formation for offensive role across the LC which is mountainous terrain. The Parliament resolution to recover the POJK territories was never translated into the defence architecture of the nation by the Executive. Declaring intent without developing the capabilities has been our historical bane.

Commencement of raising of a specialised mountain corps for offensive defence in the mountains, still ongoing for over five years due to paucity of funds, and now the reorientation of one of the mobile corps for employment in the mountains addresses to a great extent this lacuna in strategic thought and intent.

The Integrated Battle Groups, which shall be the teeth of these corps, need to be innovatively equipped with high technology weapons and equipment to create and exploit a non-linear battlefield matrix.

Tour of Duty (TOD)

The armed forces have floated a trial balloon for implementing the 'TOD' concept as an additional avenue for entry into the Armed Forces. The concept aims to synthesise the needs of the armed forces and the central governance.

The Armed Forces want a leaner, meaner, and younger fighting force, release from internal security role to focus on new age warfare, technological up-gradation of manpower, and equipment and combat structure in tune to fight the wars of the future.

The government looks to a reduced armed force human resource expenditure to release more funds for capital expenditure, professional up-gradation of CAPF to release armed forces from an internal security role, assure high qualitative requirement of manpower for armed forces, in tune with combat requirements of the future, and assist in nation-building by preparing a wide base of disciplined and dynamic manpower for lateral absorption into the Central governance structure, industry management and entrepreneur roles.

However, the concept has generated expected resistance from entrenched interests in the armed forces and central bureaucracy hierarchies.

'TOD' volunteers would be the right resource for the armed forces in the long run. They will bring in much needed technologically savvy manpower, keep its war fighting profile young, and seed the governance environment and industry with greater awareness and sensitivities to its needs.

The government has adequate political will and capital to push through the expected resistance from entrenched interests in the armed forces and central bureaucratic hierarchies. The knowledgeable entrenched interests, as has happened so many times in the past, are imaginative enough to wreck these reforms through weak drafting of the Government Order and critical loopholes in the accompanying Rules for exploiting to derail the reforms during implementation.

The government shall perforce have to exercise intimate political supervision to ensure its success. (20)

Make in Bharat

The all too well-known weakness of the country's R&D setup compels the nation to meet its need for state of art weapons and equipment through recourse to foreign manufacturers. But this path has its own severe demerits of reliability in supplies of equipment and spares, heavy economic outflow,

and most critical factor of susceptibility to embedded malware in weapon software programmes.

Self-sufficiency in domestic manufacturing of software predominant equipment is the way out. The new policy of the Government to push 'Make in Bharat' for self-reliance in defence and involvement of the private sector in the manufacture of high technology weapon platforms is just the step required.

Revolutionary reforms do take time to show results and need to be persevered. The production of K 9 artillery guns, development of advanced technology handheld weapons, production-ready design of 'see-through armour' and all-round all-weather vision for armoured fighting vehicles, undertaking time-bound development of revolutionary wingman technology enabled Tejas Mark II, hypervelocity missiles, and weapon grade directed energy weapons, strongly indicate to the nation choosing the right path to self-reliance in defence technology and production.

PART IV

Appendices & Bibliography

Appendix 'A': Bogey of Military Coup in India

We the people of India do solemnly resolve to constitute India…assuring the dignity of the individual and the unity and integrity of the Nation.

– Constitution of India

General

One of the most insidious theories propounded to keep the military undermined within the governance structure of the Republic of India has been to periodically raise the bogey of a military coup.

Prominent strategic and military analysts within the country have expressed their views from time to time, in well-articulated critiques, about the improbability of a military coup in India or rather of it being a non-issue. These thinkers have based their views upon critical aspects of the most rigorous due diligence process followed for selection of the three service chiefs with inputs from multifarious security and intelligence agencies, armed forces to population ratio, a plethora of intelligence and Para Military Forces, broad spectrum of regional representation, size and vastness of territorial spread of the country, strong democratic traditions of the nation and finally, but not the least, the historical track record of political aloofness of the armed forces. These all combined would preclude any eventuality of a military coup.

However, the bogey of a military coup has been kept alive and continues to raise its ugly head from time to time. There is only one plausible answer and it's extremely unflattering to the mandarins of South Block. It is **to keep the political class wary of dealing with the armed forces of their own nation!**

To seek clear answers to this dichotomy, the subject at hand needs to be addressed from a broader perspective.

Statement of the Problem

The Constitution of India may be termed as a sacred legal, social, cultural and governance contract between the Citizen of India and the people responsible for manning the governance structure of the country from time to time. A coup by the military would be an assault on the constitution itself. Whereas, there are **ample institutional checks and balances in our governance system to prevent a military coup in India** the subject continues to raise its head from time to time. This should logically lead the cognoscenti to search for answers to the following questions:-

What are the checks and balances for safeguarding the Constitution of India?

Are the armed forces of India a threat to the Constitution of the nation? Whether yes or no, are they the only threat?

What could be the broad spectrum of threats to the Constitution of India?

What is the historical perspective, since independence, on the issues raised?

What could be the probable causes for raising the bogey of a military coup in India time and again?

Checks and Balances for Safeguarding the Constitution of India

The Constitution of India has entrusted the Executive, i.e. the Government of India, with the task of ensuring the safety and integrity of the constitution against external as well as an internal threat.

The Constitution has further laid down a fine system of division of powers and responsibilities between the three organs of state the Executive, the Legislature and the Judiciary thereby ensuring that no one organ of the state becomes supreme and poses a threat to the Constitution itself.

This system is further buttressed by key autonomous Constitutional functionaries such as the Comptroller and Auditor General of India, the Election Commission, and the Chief Information Commissioner. These constitutional functionaries perform the critical role of independent watchdogs on the functioning of the state.

The system is further subject to public scrutiny through a 'free press', an informal 'Fourth Estate'.

Any attempt at disrupting these systems of checks and balances may therefore be construed as the first attempt at subversion of the Constitution.

Military Threats to the Constitution of India

Nominally the President of India is the Supreme Commander of the Armed Forces. However, the Government of India exercises control over its armed forces through the MoD, heavily staffed by civil bureaucracy. The three Armed Forces Service Headquarters have been amalgamated into the MoD only in January 2020.

The three armed forces service chiefs exercise staff control only over their respective service. The actual operational command over the troops vests with the C-in-Cs of respective Theatres. Thus, a 'meeting of minds' of a diverse body of key high appointments has to take place to enable subversion of the constitution by the military. The fact that all military personnel take an oath to safeguard the Constitution and also to obey only lawful command of their superiors further reduces the risk of such a 'meeting of minds' taking place. The existence of a plethora of security and intelligence agencies under the Ministry of Home to monitor against such an eventuality further obviates such an occurrence.

However, any system of governance is as good or bad as the people staffing it. **Theoretically speaking, therefore, the possibility of subversion of the Constitution of India by the Indian armed forces is as improbable or probable as from within the Executive itself.**

The periodic threat perception of a military coup may therefore be traced to the 'Us versus Them' syndrome, the root cause of which lay in excluding the Service Headquarters from the MoD structure. Looking dispassionately, **the most effective way of exercising control over the armed forces would be by integrating their service headquarters into an integrated MoD structure.** This aspect, incidentally, had been recommended by almost all task forces created to recommend restructuring the national defence structure to make it more cohesive.

Broad Spectrum of Threats to our Constitution

Threat to the Constitution of India can be broadly categorized as emerging from external and internal factors.

External political, commercial, and religious interests/ entities by employing force or threat of use of force in conjunction with internal factors compliant to their interests. (The religious spectrum is intentionally mentioned as in the recorded history of mankind maximum casualties and atrocities have been inflicted in conflicts attributable to religious reasons.)

Internal political, commercial, and religious interests/ entities, in consonance with 'committed'/compliant persona engaged in governance, through internal subversion.

Historical Perspective

Since the country's independence on 15 August 1947 there have been no recorded assaults or attempts to subvert the Constitution of India through a military coup by the country's armed forces.

Imposition of 'Emergency' in the late Seventies, with consequential growth of extra-judicial power centers may be deemed to be an attempt at subverting the Constitution of India. The role played in this act by the then elected political class in governance, duly supported by 'committed/compliant constitutional authorities and bureaucratic setup is all too well documented.

Overall, six Acts passed by the Parliament, from time to time, have been struck down by the Supreme Court, either in part or in full, for violating the doctrine of Basic Structure of the Constitution.

Various attempts, from time to time, in whittling down the autonomy and authority of constitutional organisations so essential in ensuring desired checks and balances vital for safeguarding the Constitution of India, have all emanated from the political class in power, duly supported by 'committed'/compliant government functionaries.

The Indian military has consistently proved its apolitical nature over the last more than seventy years. Attempts at politicizing the military hierarchy, seen from this prism of history, would be tantamount to tinkering with a system that has stood the test of time. **'Committed'/compliant Chief(s) of the armed forces would increase rather than decrease the probability of subversion of the Constitution from within.**

Probable Causes for Bogey of Military Coup

India is a mature democracy. In no other mature democracy do we have this sorry spectacle where the integrity and loyalty of its armed forces is called into question time and again. The **armed forces** of the country are currently one of the few constitutional organisations **'committed'/compliant to the Constitution of India** rather than to the political dispensation in power.

Under the given circumstances there is no tangible physical cause to **explain the raising of the bogey of a military coup. Some possible causes** may be deduced as under:-

- The psychological feeling of insecurity fed by the 'us versus them' syndrome.
- To mask real intention to weaken and hobble military hierarchy to make it more committed'/compliant.
- To divert attention from the dispensation that may be the real threat to a subversion of our constitution.

Postscript

The integrity and safety of our nation is intricately linked to its Constitution and cannot be compromised with. Towards that end, the creation of the DMA is a step in the right direction. Hopefully it will lay to rest the bogey of military coup, once and for all. Nevertheless, it needs to be mentioned that any future attempts at raising the bogey of military coup are dealt with seriously, as they are tantamount to adversely impacting the functional efficiency of the external security infrastructure of the nation.

It would be apt to reiterate that any attempts to impose a 'committed/compliant' military hierarchy would be a self-defeating proposition and should be severely discouraged.

Appendix 'B': Thrust & Logic of Chinese Foreign Policy

Author's Note

*(Even during my school days, I found reading books on military campaigns very interesting. Subsequently as a student of history during my graduate and postgraduate years I found the history of China, Japan, and Tibet highly fascinating. The 1990s was the time when the Indian strategic establishment started shifting its focus from Pakistan to look at China as the long-term threat. It came naturally to me to **write this article, in 1993,** based on almost two decades of my insight on the subject.)*

THRUST & LOGIC OF CHINESE FOREIGN POLICY

By Maj RS Sidhu, SM

*(First published in Trishul, a Triservice journal of Defence Services Staff College Wellington (India), Volume VI No 2 – **January 1994**, and reproduced with their kind permission.)*

Introduction

For centuries, China regarded herself as the Central Flowery Kingdom, the only 'Civilisation' on Earth, and its ruler as T'ien-Tzu, the Son of Heaven. There has been a two thousand years old tradition to view China as the centre of the Universe. All the Chinese leaders from Sun Yat-Sen to Chiang Kai-Shek to Mao Tse-Dong, down to Deng share the belief in the greatness of China. Infact, it was Sun Yat-Sen, rather than the communists, as popularly believed, who first advocated that China assume a greater responsibility towards the world by articulating "...... we must aid the weaker and smaller peoples to oppose the Greater Powers". The traditional China believed itself to be the repository of unique values that ought to be accepted by all mankind. This traditional belief amongst her people continues even today and has a bearing on her political thinking and foreign policy. The difficulty of modern China in adjusting to the fast-changing international comity of nations is partly explained by this factor.

Search for a Modern Ideology by China

The history of China's confrontation with the West clearly shows that the Chinese search for a new ideology was the result of deep national frustration at the inadequacy of the traditional Confucian ideology and socio-political system to cope with the powerful challenge of the West at the turn of this century.

Rejection of Democracy

To meet the challenge posed by the West and to solve their own national problems, the Chinese could only turn to Western ideologies. Democracy was perfunctorily tried but it did not fit into the traditional Chinese framework and failed.

Meeting Points of Communism and Confucianism

Communism had in it many important elements of the traditional Chinese socio-political order:-

- A centralised regime.
- A conformist ideology.
- Ruling elite well versed in scriptures.
- Lastly, and most important, it had a universal vision.

Thus, the Communist ideology and political system, besides being modern and having the advantage of multi-point contact with traditional China, also carried with it the promise of restoring China its traditional universal role.

Adoption of Communism for Advancement of China's National Aims

The communist movement grew under the shadow of growing national indignation against the Western Powers and Japan. The war against Japan enabled the communists to mobilise the masses and work up their patriotic fervour. The communist success against the KMT was in no small measure due to their skilful propaganda denigrating the Nationalist Party as a stooge of imperialism. The Chinese Communists had thus largely conceived their struggle in nationalist terms. Infact, Mao's ascendancy in the

Communist movement represented the triumph of the nationalist aspect of communism. Therefore, the movement in China, though inspired by the Communist ideology and Russian example, was essentially a nationalist growth aimed at China's regeneration. The subsequent break by the Chinese communist from the international movement under Russian leadership, further emphasises this point. It is immaterial today whether the Communist ruling elite of China sees their struggle as an ideological or historical one, because by now ideology in their minds has become indistinguishable from nationalism. Indeed, communism and nationalism have attained a near – perfect fusion in China.

Foreign Policy Objectives of Modern China

- **Global Objectives.** The greatest desire of China has been to build for herself a position of prestige through the development of economic and military strength and to exercise effective political influence and power on the world stage. Thus, the ultimate aim of communist China is to bring about proletarian revolution through people's war. In realpolitik terms, to achieve a Great Power status.

- **Nuclear Weapons and Blue Water Navy.** China has ample historical experience to realise that no nation can attain a superpower status without a strong nuclear armoury and blue water navy. It is for this reason that China has been single-mindedly building up its nuclear forces and an ocean-going navy despite all its economic problems.

- **Economic Power.** The Communist Chinese hierarchy is aware of the twin principles that 'power flows from the barrel of the gun' and 'money purchases the gun'. Towards this end, China has been studiously building up her economy. After initially dropping the 'Bamboo Curtain', vital to ensure the very survival of Communism in China and also to protect her nascent industries from foreign competition, the Communists have been steadily entering the world economic system. The 'Great Leap Forward' under Mao and the recent ' Four Modernisations' programme under Deng are cases in point. China is determined to back up her thrust towards achieving a superpower status with economic strength. The fact of the Chinese economy presently being the most dynamic and fastest-growing, coupled with her having developed a huge trade surplus with the US, are indicators of the success achieved by her in this sphere.

- **Regional Objectives.** As a pre-requisite towards the attainment of superpower status, it is imperative that China establishes her predominance in the Asian region. Towards this end the Chinese policy in this region is aimed at:-

- **Establishing Hegemony.** In realpolitik terms read as suzerainty, in the region adjoining her borders. This includes any region ever ruled by any ruler of China. Witness the annexation of Tibet, part of Spratley Islands, the Ussuri river dispute with USSR, the Mac-

Mohan Line border dispute with India and laying claims of suzerainty on large tracts of areas in various South East Asian countries adjacent to her borders. In these ventures, China has met with only partial success due to a lack of a modern army and a comparatively weak economy. Hence, her temporary abandonment of expansionist plans and instituting a modernisation plan for her armed forces and economy before continuing afresh.

- **Prevent the establishment of any rival centre of power in the region.** Witness the Chinese opposition to the establishment of US influence in the region by fighting a proxy war against it in Korea in the early fifties and aiding North Vietnam against the US in the sixties and seventies; destroying India's influence in the region by one stroke in the 1962 war; attempt to cow down Vietnam by a so-called punitive action in the eighties.

- Attain influence in the region through economic ties and export of weapons and technology, especially with nations inimical to the interest of USA.

Tactical Shifts in Policy. In pursuit of their international strategy, the Chinese Communists have quite often changed their tactics. These tactical shifts are designed to promote the basic Chinese strategy of establishing a world order whose centre is Beijing, by ensuring that the country at no time is forced to fight a two-front war. Consequently, China has gone in for temporary friendships/alliances with individual countries as dictated by political compulsions of given situations. China has never hesitated to cast off such temporary shifts as soon as they outlive their utility as evidenced by the following:-

Sino-USSR Brotherhood. To attain power in Beijing the Communists had to fight against the USA backed Chiang Kai-Shek. Thus, initially, friendship with USSR was necessary not only to secure its rear but also to receive Russian aid in strengthening her economy and armed forces. But China was averse to playing second fiddle to USSR. Hence, when the Western threat receded, the Chinese broke off with USSR over ideological and territorial differences.

- **Sino-Indian Bhai Bhaism.** The need to keep her Southern flank secure while fighting the Western-backed Chiang Kai-Shek was reason enough to initially establish friendship with India. However, giving refuge to the Dalai Lama of Tibet by India after the annexation of Tibet by China, coupled with border differences and growing influence of India in international for a were sufficient reasons for China to break-off this short lived friendship by invading India in 1962.

- **Sino-Vietnamese Break.** The Chinese initially supported North Vietnam to oppose the establishment of US influence in the region. However, the increased stature of Vietnam in the region, after the military withdrawal of the US, was perceived by China as inimical to its interest in the region. Vietnam's alliance with USSR was also viewed as being aimed at reducing her influence in the region. The above two factors, coupled with China's view of Vietnam being its vassal state in the historical past, resulted in China launching its abortive punitive action against Vietnam in the eighties.

- **Sino-Japanese Relations.** China's historical enmity with Japan is by now legendary. The latter is still viewed by China as one of the major threats to itself. But this has not prevented the Chinese hierarchy from seeking friendly relations with Japan, initially to secure its Eastern flank from the Russian threat, and subsequently to gain access to Japanese funds and technology in an attempt to bolster its economy.

- **Sino-US Rapprochement.** The US attempts at establishing its influence in the region coupled with its support to Chiang Kai-Shek in China caused the latter to enter into a proxy war with the US in Korea in the fifties and Vietnam in the sixties and seventies. However, the break with USSR forced China to reconsider its relations with the US. Thus, China entered into a rapprochement with its erstwhile numero uno enemy not only to use it as a countervailing force against USSR but also to obtain modern technology, funds and influence to enter the world trading system so as to modernise and strengthen its own economy and military strength.

Likely Effects of Breakup of USSR on Chinese Policy

The breakup of the USSR is bound to have a profound effect on Chinese policy as it has not only reduced the threat on its Western borders, but has also resulted in a power vacuum readymade for being stepped into by China.

- The break-up of the USSR due to economic reasons will further reinforce the Chinese determination to strengthen her economy at all costs. Thus, economic recovery will be the main propulsion of Chinese policy vis-a-vis territorial ambitions in the near future.

- A USA dominated unipolar world can retard the Chinese drive towards economic strength. Hence, China is likely to adopt a low profile internationally till she feels herself to have become strong enough to challenge US power on equal terms.

- China's thrust in future will be power politics at low key with special emphasis on economic dependence by:-

  - Allowing regional countries a slice of the Chinese market on the one hand and investing in critical sectors of economies of other countries, on the other.
  - Aid to underdeveloped countries to wean them from Western dependence.

Likely Chinese Policy towards India In The Near Future. The world situation is once again leading China towards it's by now customary, tactical shifts in foreign policy. The following factors are likely to influence China in adopting a softer line towards India in the near future:-

- The disintegration of USSR has removed a major threat to China from across the Western border. But the resultant instability in this Muslim dominated region coupled with a volatile Muslim population in its province of Sinkiang, which borders this region, is giving Chinese leaders unease.

- China requires a period of relative peace on its borders so as to enable its economic restructuring and modernisation of industry and the armed forces to be put into effect without any external interference.

- China perceives a reduced threat from India at this juncture owing to the latter's preoccupation with her economic restructuring, safeguarding own integrity from separatist militant movements within her own borders and an aggressive Pakistan waiting on the sidelines to take advantage of the situation, aided and gently goaded by China.

- Deterioration of the geopolitical situation in the Asian sub-continent may induce US intervention in the region, which would go against long term Chinese interests in the region.

Likely Long-Term Chinese Policy towards India. Thus, any softening in the Chinese stance towards India should be viewed by the latter in the correct perspective and should not be taken to signal any change in the long-term policy objective of China towards India. It would be more in the form of short-term tactical deviation to tide over the compulsions of the existing economic and geo-political situation. China would feel free to revert to its original policy course once the geopolitical situation is again in her favour. An economically vibrant and militarily far more powerful China will be a greater threat to India in the long-term, especially in view of its nuclear superpower status.

Conclusion

As in the historical past, the Chinese Communist today visualise China as the originator of a superior doctrine and political system which other countries would do well to accept in their own interest. Thus, seen from a historical perspective, the basic thrust of the Chinese foreign policy has always been a compulsive urge to reassert China's imperial grandeur.

Appendix 'C': Understanding China

(First published by Centre for Joint Warfare Studies, New Delhi in January 2020 **UNDERSTANDING CHINA** and reproduced with their kind permission.)

Measures undertaken by a nation to overcome its strategic weaknesses are themselves the most lucrative and natural target for an opponent.

— **Ibid**

The Myth of China as a Monolithic Colossus

This critique is aimed at peering deep inside the outer façade of China as a monolithic colossus, to understand the psyche and dilemmas underlying Chinese compulsions, impelling it onto the path it is currently travelling on.

China today is one of the major global power in terms of geopolitical influence. Certainly, in its near vicinity it strides like a colossus. Or so it seems to the untrained eye. Looked at critically, **at this juncture**, the following emerges:-

- Existence of deep geographical, demographic, and economic fault lines.
- Lack of reckonable allies. North Korea and Pakistan do not meet the criteria of being 'reckonable'.
- Inadequate blue water navy to establish sea control over its extended maritime lifelines beyond the SCS.
- Countries inimical to its desired global image block its maritime aspirations – formidable countries such as the US, Japan, and India by virtue of their geographical locations/geopolitical power.
- The much vaunted 'String of Pearls" enables it just peacetime visibility. Its efficacy to withstand the rigours of active operations, to say the least, is doubtful.
- China's dilemma is evidenced by it being forced to undertake US Dollar 800 billion gambles in BRI.
- China's BRI and ongoing actions in the SCS should be seen not as its strength but as its acceptance of its maritime vulnerability.
- The ongoing debilitating trade war with the US is further putting severe strain on its economy.
- Uncharacteristic inhibition of Chinese leadership in the use of overwhelming force, a la Tiananmen Square, to overcome overt display of people's opposition in Hong Kong, despite the severe loss of face, is to be seen as an indicator of its current economic vulnerability.

However, the above also undeniably verifies China's push for a China-centric world, the basic thrust of its deep rooted national aspiration for centuries.

THE CHINESE WORLD VISION

The Collective Psyche of China

For centuries, China has regarded herself as the Central Flowery Kingdom, the only 'Civilisation' on Earth, and its ruler as T'ien-Tzu, the Son of Heaven. The Chinese continue to view their country as the fulcrum around which geopolitics must rotate. A strong and confident China must hold sway over all the regions ever part of China or under Chinese suzerainty at any point of history. It is this historic urge, embedded deep into the collective Chinese psyche, which to a great extent explains their inability to peacefully adjust to the established international environment. **As in the historical past, the basic thrust of the Chinese policy is the compulsive urge to reassert China's imperial grandeur.**

Fusion of Traditional Chinese Aspirations and Communist Ideology

The occupation of China, initially by Western powers and subsequently Japan, led to an outgrowth of nationalist spirit amongst the Chinese people. By portraying the then KMT Government as a stooge of foreign powers, it enabled the Chinese Communist Party to spread its tentacles amongst the peasantry and mobilise them to regain national honour. A centralised regime, armed with a conformist ideology, with a universal vision provided the ideal vehicle to achieve the traditional Chinese urge of once again being the centre of world civilisation.

The Chinese Communists thus largely couched their movement in nationalist terms aimed at China's regeneration. The subsequent break by Communist China from the Russian led Communist International movement, further emphasises this point. There is seamless fusion today between communism and nationalism within China. **The concomitant one-party rule ensures not only ideological continuity, but also unhindered long-term planning to realise their geostrategic aim of a China-centric world order.**

FAULT LINES WITHIN CHINA
Geographical Composition of China

China is bordered to its south by the South East Asian countries of Vietnam and Laos followed by Myanmar. To its south-west China is bordered by India, Bhutan, Nepal, POJK and Afghanistan across the Himalayas and the Tibetan plateau. To its west lie the Central Asian countries of Tajikistan, Kazakhstan, and Kirgizstan. Mongolia and Russia border China on the north with North Korea lying to its north-east.

China's more than 14500 kilometres long coastline on the east and south-east overlooks the Yellow Sea, East China Sea and SCS. **South Korea and Japan lying across the Yellow Sea dominate Chinese access to the open seas from the north-east. Japan and Taiwan dominate its access to**

open seas across the East China Sea. China's access to open seas across the SCS is dominated by Taiwan, the Philippines, and other South East Asian countries.

China is bounded by the sea to its east; thick tropical forests to its south-east, very high mountains of the Tibetan plateau and Xinjiang to its south-west and west; cold desert and arid grasslands of Inner Mongolia and Manchuria to its north. These regions are arid, having less than 40 centimetres of annual precipitation, and have very harsh terrain and climate. **They, however, provide an effective natural barrier or buffer for land access to mainland China.** Encompassed by these formidable physical barriers lies the mainland of China comprising fertile river plains and lowlands, with good precipitation, in its east and south-central regions. **This forms the core of China.**

The sea to the east provides the easiest access to mainland China.

Northern, western and south-western regions of China having very forbidding landscape, harsh climate and limited rainfall are inhospitable for human habitation and agriculture. Despite its vast geographical stretch, **only 15% of China's land surface is suitable for cultivation.**

The mainland of China is well served by two great rivers, the **Yellow River** in the North, and the **Yangtze** River to the South. These rivers originate from the Tibetan plateau. The drainage-basins of these two rivers, though forming just 22% of its landmass, are home to 60% population of China. Pearl River in South China, the second largest river of China also originates in the Tibetan Plateau.

Hence, the Tibetan plateau is critical to the water security of China.

Demographics

China has an overall population of 1.4 billion, but its geographical spread is highly uneven. Its population is concentrated in the east because of geographical factors. 60% of its population is concentrated in just 22% of its landmass. Its eastern and south-central regions, forming the core, have an approximate population of 770 million with an average population density of approximately 430 per kilometre square. **In this sense, China is actually a relatively narrow country, with an extremely dense population.**

The population is most sparse in the mountainous, desert, and grassland regions of the northwest and southwest. In Inner Mongolia Autonomous Region, portions are completely uninhabited.

South-western region, comprising Tibet has an approximate population of 190 million with an average population density of 80 per kilometres square. Though this region is now dominated by Han Chinese, **Tibet is potentially unstable and is vulnerable to outside influences.**

North-western region, comprising Xinjiang, has an approximate population of 100 million with an average population density of 30 per kilometres square. Though this region is now also dominated by Han Chinese, the **ethnic population of Xinjiang is predominantly Muslim, with a significant ongoing insurgency.**

Northern region, comprising Inner Mongolia, has an approximate population of 160 million with an average population density of 105 per kilometres square. The region is stable.

North Eastern region, comprising Manchuria, has an approximate population of 110 million with an average population density of 140 per kilometre square. **Manchuria is also stable and of all four buffers is the most integrated with the Chinese core.**

91% of China's population is of Han ethnic origin. The remainder 9% are ethnic minorities. The next largest ethnic groups in terms of population include the Zhuang – 17 million, Manchu – 10 million, Hui – 10 million, Miao – 9 million, Uighur – 9 million, Yi – 9 million, Tujia – 8 million, Mongols – 6 million, Tibetans – 6 million, Buyei – 3 million, Yao – 3 million, and Koreans – 3 million. **These are sizable numbers having questionable affinity to the central government.**

Interestingly, whereas **the core of China is overwhelmingly Han, its outlying regions are predominantly of diverse ethnicity, with major security connotations.** To overcome its perceived security concerns the Chinese Government is implementing a policy of altering the long-term demographic pattern of the outlying regions through the coercive settlement of Han Chinese. The Han Chinese being relocated in these inhospitable terrains is unhappy and there is a high rate of withdrawal amongst them. **This is further alienating the people of its border regions.**

Due to geographical limitations of inhospitable terrain and climate, the western regions of China have always been at a severe economic disadvantage vi-a-vis the eastern regions. High elevations, sharp slopes, extreme cold climate, low precipitation, distance from the coast all combine to make the western regions relatively unviable for agrarian and industrial commerce. The shift from the traditional agrarian economy to an industrial economy has further sharpened the economic and social divides within China. The demands of an exceptionally high industrial economic growth have fuelled new population concentrations in coastal metropolises on the one hand and increased income disparity between the rich and poor on the other.

The resultant increase in income disparity between the eastern and western regions, urban and rural areas, the rich and poor in metropolises is causing social unrest. This is one of the most dangerous fault lines within China.

The idea that is China

60% of China's population, concentrated in just 22% of its territory, in a roughly 1000 kms wide arc along the seacoast represents **the core of China and is overwhelmingly of Han ethnic origin.** This arc, containing almost a billion people, is one of the most densely populated regions of the world.

The far-flung autonomous regions of Tibet, Xinjiang, Inner Mongolia, Qinghai, and Gansu comprise 55% of the country's landmass but contain only 7% of its population. These thinly populated regions, predominantly comprising ethnic minorities are deemed to be the buffer regions to the mainland Han Chinese core. Many of these minorities have doubtful loyalty to China, strained relations with the central government, and active cross-border ties with neighbouring countries. **Thus, we see that geographically a good part of what we think of as China is not ethnically Chinese.**

China has regional variations in religious affiliation of its population. The Tibetans are Buddhists, whereas the Uighurs in Xingjian follow the Muslim faith. Roughly 60% Han population officially are atheists, while the balance believes in various forms of folk religion.

There are severe divides within the Han Chinese as well:-

- Urban – rural
- Rich – poor
- Northern plains – Southern plains

The diversity of these group interests within Han China has frequently led to fragmentation and civil war.

Historical Backdrop

The inland borders of China are mostly mountainous and cold, difficult to garrison, and populated by minority peoples of doubtful loyalty to the central government. Its **borders are easier to invade than to defend**. Traditionally China's maritime interests have remained mostly limited to coastal waters even though the **long coastline provides easiest access to the mainland China**.

Historically, threats to China's Han core have originated in the highlands. To guard against overland invasion successive Chinese rulers have sought to push the Core's borders outward, integrating these highlands as strategic buffer zones forming a protective shield around the core.

To be secure, China must control the buffer regions. But maintaining control of these regions, in turn, requires a strong and united core. And that means overcoming immense internal divisions – not only between Northern and Southern region river plains of Yellow and Yangtze rivers, but also smaller regional units, each with their own geography, history, dialect, and interests.

Chinese history is defined by cycles of unity and fragmentation, from periods when a strong Han core captures and holds the surrounding buffers to those when a weak core breaks into its constituent parts, loses internal coherence and cedes control of the highlands.

It was around 200 BC that the Chinese mainland was first unified under the Han dynasty. This was followed by a period of strife till the Chinese empire first extended control over territories in Central Asia in the 8th and 9th centuries, under the Tang dynasty. Thereafter in the 14th century China was under Mongol rule for almost 90 years. It was in the 17th and 18th century that Tibet, Mongolia, and Xinjiang were first annexed. A weakened Chinese empire was, thereafter, defeated by the Western powers in the two opium wars of the 19th century. This led to a century of foreign domination, first by the Western powers and subsequently by the Japanese. It was only after the close of the Second World War that China could again control its own destiny. Subsequently, Tibet was again annexed in 1950.

Subsequent to the establishment of CCP rule, a resurgent China has used force in its neighbourhood as under:-

- Forcible annexation of Tibet in 1950.
- Against USA led UN forces in Korea in 1951-53.
- Crushing of Tibetan independence movement in 1952.
- Border war against India in 1962.
- Punitive border action against India at Nathu La in 1967.
- Ussuri River island conflict against USSR in 1968.
- Forcible occupation of island territory from Vietnam in Paracel Islands, in the SCS in 1974.
- Punitive border action against Vietnam in 1979.
- Forcible occupation of island territory in Spratley Islands, in the SCS from Vietnam in 1988.
- Forcible occupation of Mischief Reef, in the SCS, from the Philippines in 1995.

In addition to the above use of force, China has resorted to threats of use of force internationally on numerous occasions. Currently it is engaged in the use of force by setting up a maritime defensive zone in the SCS in disputed waters, wherein its actions have been ruled as violating international laws by the International Court of Justice.

Economic

There has been a very high growth rate of the Chinese economy during the past two decades. This very rapid growth rate has led to:-

- Setting up of manufacturing industries
- Reorientation of trade and commerce activities from traditional Silk land routes to maritime trade.
- Demand for external resources.
- Coming up of new highly dense population centres with floating population creating a new demographic challenge for the central authorities.

However, the increasing maritime trade and industrial centres are perforce concentrated along China's 14,500 kilometres long eastern coastline. The interiors of the west with high elevations, extreme cold conditions and long distances from the coast make land transport infrastructure an economically prohibitive alternative making the industrial product uncompetitive in the international market. Apart from creating new demographic fissures, this has also resulted in extending the core of mainland China right to the exposed eastern coastline, making it extremely vulnerable to foreign maritime threat.

Geographically the easiest access to mainland China is through its eastern coastline. The demands of competitive industrial output and international trade have forced China to locate its most vital assets in its exposed maritime underbelly. Creating a maritime buffer along its exposed 14,500 kilometres eastern coastline has introduced a paradigm shift to China's geostrategic challenge of managing its external security.

Strategic Dilemmas of China
Maritime Vulnerability

Geography has gifted to China its biggest geostrategic dilemma, a classic case of being hemmed in 'Between the Devil and the Deep Sea'. **Maritime trade is critical to China to survive as a major economic and geostrategic powerhouse**. On one hand, the massive geographical barriers to its North-South-West make land trade prohibitively uneconomical and also make it vulnerable as they pass through regions that are politically unstable and volatile. On other hand, while China's access to open seas is dominated by countries inimical to its interest, the **14,500 kilometres long coastline is vulnerable to maritime threat**. Its major rival, the US, is the pre-eminent maritime power dominating China's maritime trade routes in the Pacific and the Indian Oceans.

China's maritime actions in the SCS are an attempt by it to create a maritime buffer zone to provide security to its extended coastline, the hub of its economic and demographic centre of gravity. But these actions have also brought it into a direct conflict of interest with all its maritime neighbours, thereby opening the doors to US interference and providing cause for India and Japan to realign themselves alongside the US to thwart Chinese bellicosity.

The ongoing debilitating trade war between China and the US and the maritime standoff between the two in the SCS has the potential of blowing into a military confrontation. In such an eventuality, win or lose, Chinese maritime trade will be the first casualty. This by itself is likely to lead to internal instability and give rise to fissiparous forces against central rule.

Chinese propensity to use force or threat to use force has created an antagonistic relationship with two other major Asian powers, India, and Japan. With an aim to secure its northern and south-western flanks, China has propped up North Korea and Pakistan as nuclear armed states with a view to neutralising Japan and India, respectively. It also gives it leverage against the US by diverting the latter's energy and attention towards nuclear proliferation.

This strategy is now unravelling. The Chinese threat has forced Japan to shed its 70 years old policy of pacifism and commence rearmament. In India a right-wing nationalist party government has hardened its stand against Chinese threats and shifted focus to its northern borders against China, with strategic support from the US. An informal alliance between the US, India, and Japan is maturing into the worst nightmare for China.

Effective Strategic Options

China is attempting to overcome this dilemma by exercising two options. The first is to open land trade routes to energy producing regions in West Asia and Central Asia, the BRI. Secondly, to establish permanent naval presence along its maritime routes, the 'String of Pearls' strategy. The strategies are inherently flawed and should be seen as a measure of China's acceptance of its maritime vulnerability.

The CPEC passes through disputed POJK region, and Sindh and Baluchistan provinces of Pakistan which are insurgency prone. CPEC is within easy strategic reach of India, hence, prone to interdiction in times of hostilities. Similar is the case with the CMEC. The economic corridor to Central Asian and West Asian regions shall pass through the volatile Xinjiang province and the highly volatile Central Asian republics. With a strong US presence in West Asia, it will again be vulnerable to interdiction during hostilities. The current projected costs of these enterprises are estimated at US Dollar 800 billion and given their survivability, it reflects a measure of the desperation of China to come out of its geostrategic dilemma.

The 'String of Pearls' is equally unviable as its efficacy to withstand an open hostility environment is questionable as China does not have the maritime resources to control the maritime trade routes passing through the Pacific Ocean and the Indian Ocean bottlenecks dominated by Japan, India, and the US.

Orientation of Chinese Armed Forces

The biggest bulwark against internal threat to CCP rule and the biggest threat to their continuity in power are the Chinese armed forces. Supreme control over the Chinese armed forces lies with the CCP. This supremacy is ensured through political interface at all levels down to the unit. The command supremacy lies with the political commissars. A conformist attitude and political indoctrination in the army hierarchy gets priority over professionalism.

The primary responsibility of the armed forces is therefore to safeguard the political hierarchy from its own people. Safeguarding the borders from external threat is secondary. This perforce inhibits the Chinese armed forces from developing its full combat potential against external adversaries. Joint warfare command and control structures, vital for the success of overseas military operations, are inadequately organised owing to the above reasons. Hence the combat potential of its armed forces beyond the immediate vicinity of its borders is uncertain.

Current Geostrategic Situation of China

Global Aspiration. It is progressively developing its economic and military strength to enable the exercise of pre-eminent geostrategic influence and power on the world stage. However, its propensity for belligerence in its immediate neighbourhood is propelling regional countries into forming strong alliances to thwart Chinese geostrategic designs.

Regional Objectives. The influence of China is truly established as the pre-eminent power in Asia. The Shanghai Security Cooperation Organisation (SSCO) is the instrument of projection of Chinese influence in the Central Asian region primarily to secure energy supplies for her ever-expanding economy. ASEAN and other countries in the region, right up to Australia, are sensitive to Chinese interests. But the commencement of rearmament by Japan, India's strategic reorientation, and pivot to the Pacific by the US are likely to adversely impact Chinese geopolitical influence.

Control over Maritime Trade Routes. Currently, it has the third largest nuclear stockpile and an ocean going navy with two indigenously manufactured aircraft carriers scheduled to join service in near future. The naval strength is, however, inadequate to implement its 'String of Pearls' strategy to safeguard its maritime trade routes, even with assured naval resource increments, in the coming decade.

Economic Power. The Chinese economy is already the second largest in the world and is projected to cross the US economy in GDP terms by 2040, as per current estimation. It has also developed a huge trade surplus against the majority of large economies of the world. However, the enormous economic resources deployed towards its BRI and the ongoing trade war initiated by the US is placing tremendous strain on its economic stability.

Establishing Hegemony. With the restructuring of its economy and modernisation of armed forces, China has already commenced expansion of her sphere of influence eastwards into the SCS and the Sea of Japan with increased belligerence. This increase in belligerence is distinctly visible even along her southern regions, especially in Tibet and borders with India.

Prevent the establishment of any rival centre of power in the region. Leaving aside South Korea, Japan, Vietnam, and India all other neighbours of China have fallen under its sphere of influence, with varying degrees of subservience to Chinese interests. China continues to intimidate the countries inimical to her interests through increased show of force. This is necessitating the US to pivot to the Pacific region to countervail Chinese influence.

Sino-Russian Interests. Currently China sees a convergence of interest with Russia owing to energy supply dependency, mutual requirement of checking Islamic extremism from the Central Asian region and countervailing US power projection capabilities in Asia.

Sino-Japanese Rivalry. Japan is strategically placed to act as a bulwark against any Chinese push for dominance in the Pacific region and deny China access control along its regional maritime trade routes. China sees an increased convergence of US, Japanese, and Indian interests in countervailing the former's rise. Japan's increased military activism is also perceived as a threat by China, necessitating attempts at neutralising Japan through a show of force.

Sino-US Cold War. Despite the strong economic linkages between the Sino-US economies, there is no denying the effective cold war undercurrents between the two countries. Heavy US presence in South Korea and Japan gives it the capability to choke Chinese maritime trade at a critical juncture. Similarly, the establishment of a US presence in the Central Asian region gives it the capability to cut off China from its critical overland energy supply lines. An economically and strategically resurgent India has the capability to pose a serious threat from the south as also deny access to the Indian Ocean maritime trade routes. This leaves China with the option to continue strengthening economic engagement on the one hand and wean away India, Japan, and South Korea from US influence through a policy of carrot and stick.

Sino-India Relationship

Boundary dispute, Tibet, sharing of river waters, sourcing of energy supplies, trade and commerce are the key sources of dispute between the countries representing two diverse cultures. China also perceives India, in alliance with the US and Japan, as a stumbling block to achieving undisputed great power status. Hence, China's engagement with India is guided by efforts to wean it away from an alliance with the US through a 'carrot and stick' approach.

The Stick

Continue to prop up a nuclear Pakistan to neutralise India.

Challenge India's geostrategic space in the Indian Ocean by permanent establishment of military presence in adjoining countries, viz. Myanmar, Sri Lanka, Djibouti, and Pakistan.

Coercive projection of force along the border with India.

Undermine Indian economy by attempts at denying sources of energy and entry to critical trade blocs.

Internal sabotage through fifth columns.

The Carrot

Mutually favourable solution of the border dispute.

Collaborative engagement vis-a-vis US and EU blocs in international trade and economic fora.

Influencing World Opinion

China is subtly influencing world opinion by exercising its soft economic power to project itself as a modern, economically vibrant, monolithic state with powerful armed forces to safeguard its national interests. Investments in adversarial countries foreign media, donations and paid news space is the route being adopted by it.

Nations inimical to its interests are having a democratic form of government. It is subtly influencing electoral outcomes in interested countries through electoral donations and influencing media articles with a view to ensuring that the government formed is sensitive to China's interests.

The intention is to project larger than life image of China, a country that cannot be defeated and is capable of retaliatory action which can adversely impact the economic and physical wellbeing of common citizens. It expects to thereby mould the public opinion of targeted nations to influence their government's attempts, if any, to undertake coercive action against China. However, the mood of right-wing nationalism in the US, India, Japan, and Australia has jeopardised the success of this campaign. Unpredictability of current adversarial leaders is unsettling to China, used to craftily designed well planned responses based on the predictability of adversary actions.

(Col RS Sidhu, Sena Medal is a post graduate in History from Delhi University. While in service with the Army he has authored various articles published in reputed service journals.)

Bibliography

1. 'The World Economy: A Millennial Perspective', by Angus Maddison. Published by Development Centre Studies, Organisation for Economic Co-operation and Development (OECD), Paris.

2. 'Tibet: The Last Months of a Free Nation India Tibet Relations (1947-1962): Part 1', by Claude Arpi, Published 2017 Vij Books. 'End Of An Era', by Claude Arpi, published 2020 Vij Books. Claude Arpi, Field Marshal KM Cariappa Chair of Excellence of The United Service Institution of India, Blog (http://www.claudearpi.net/the-indian-presence-in-tibet-1947-1962), excerpt from Army Headquarters internal memorandum, "…4th Mahrattas stationed at Lebong (Darjeeling) have a Company on detachment in Gyantse in Tibet…" Brigadier (CHAND N. DAS) D.M.I. GS Branch, MT Directorate of Jul 49.

3. 'China Is A Private Sector Economy', by Peter Engardio (21 August 2005). Bloomberg Businessweek.

4. 'China's Strategic Vision, Strengths, and Vulnerabilities', Kevin Rudd's Address, 09 April 2019 at the 55th West Point Senior Conference, Asia Society Policy Institute, Washington, DC. https://

asiasociety.org/policy-institute/chinas-strategic-vision-strengths-and-vulnerabilities

5.   'The Chinese Communist Party Targets the Private Sector', by Scott Livingston, October 8, 2020, Centre For Strategic and International Studies, Washington, DC. https://www.csis.org/analysis/chinese-communist-party-targets-private-sector

6.   US Congressional Research Service Report, updated 29 December 2020 – 'U.S.-China Strategic Competition in South and East China Seas: Background and Issues for Congress'. (Congressional Research Service https://crsreports.congress.gov R42784)

7.   'The Costliest Pearl' by BertilLintner, Westland Publications

8.   'Overseas Chinese, Ethnic Minorities and Nationalism, De-Centring China' by Elena Barabantseva, published by Routledge Publishers.

9.   Chapter III of 'China and India, 2025', A Comparative Assessment Book Author(s): Charles Wolf Jr., Siddhartha Dalal, Julie DaVanzo, Eric V. Larson, AlisherAkhmedjonov, HarunDogo, Meilinda Huang and Silvia Montoya, Published by RAND Corporation.

10. 'China in the 2010s Rebalancing Growth and Strengthening Social Safety Nets', Organisation for Economic Co-operation and Development (OECD) contribution to the China Development

Forum 20-22 March 2010. https://www.oecd.org/china/44878634.pdf

11.   'China Has Two Paths To Global Domination', by Jake Sullivan, Hal Brands, Foreign Policy, 22 May 2020.

12.   'Rare Earth, Has US Lost the Technology Battle Against China?' by Brigadier V Mahalingam (Retd), published February 2021 by Vivekanand International Foundation.

13.   'ANALYSING CHINA'S DIGITAL AND SPACE BELT AND ROAD INITIATIVE' AjeyLele and Kritika Roy, Published by Institute for Defence Studies and Analyses, November 2019 ISBN: 978-93-82169-90-1

14.   'Countering China's Influence Operations: Lessons from Australia', Amy Searight, May 8, 2020 https://www.csis.org/analysis/countering-chinas-influence-operations-lessons-australia

15.   Japan Times report by Sarah cook https://www.japantimes.co.jp/opinion/2020/06/19/commentary/world-commentary/chinas-global-media-influence-grows-pushback/

16.   Business Standard, June 09 2020 12:47 IST 'Chinese mouthpiece paid US newspapers US Dollars 19 million in ads, printing: Report' https://www.business-standard.com/article/international/chinese-mouthpiece-paid-us-newspapers-19-mn-in-ads-printing-report-120060900514_1.html

17. 'China's influence over the UN', by NeelamDeo, 7 MAY 2020, Indian Council on Global Relations, Gateway House. https://www.gatewayhouse.in/chinas-influence-un/

18. This part was first published by Centre for Joint Warfare Studies, New Delhi in 'Tackling The Chinese Conundrum By India' September 2020 https://cenjows.in/article-detail?id=396and is reproduced in part with their kind permission.

19. Theatre Commands for Indian Armed Forces https://valleysandvalour.blogspot.com/20/07/theatre-commands-for-indian-armed-forces.html?m=1

20. Indarmy Tour of Duty Reforms https://cenjows.in/article-detail?id=284

Special Acknowledgement

My special thanks to Ambassador Anil Trigunayat, Distinguished Fellow of Vivekanand Research Foundation; Professor Srikanth Kondapalli, Centre for East Asian Studies Jawaharlal Nehru University; and Lt Col Naresh Bana, Treasurer and Chair Editorial Board WAPPP, for their support.

Author Profile

The author Veteran Col RS Sidhu, 65 years, has served in the army for 29 years and is a decorated war veteran who has the right credentials to write on the subject. He has a Masters degree in History from Delhi University and is an amateur 'China watcher' of more than three decades standing. His incisive and predictive analysis on events  and strategic matters has been published in magazines and journals of repute.

He is also the author of the successful book *Success from Being Mad*, about inspiring real-life stories of ten Karma Yogi Mad Veterans of Indian Armed Forces who have rousingly explored the uncharted terrain on the entrepreneur street.

He enjoys yoga and deep meditation and is passionate about offbeat adventures.